Jane's

SUPERMARINE
SPITFIRE

DAVID OLIVER

HarperCollins*Publishers*

Harper Collins*Publishers*
77–85 Fulham Palace Road
Hammersmith,
London, W6 8JB

First Published in Great Britain by
HarperCollins*Publishers* 1999

1 3 5 7 9 10 8 6 4 2

© HarperCollinsPublishers 1999

ISBN 0 00 472260 4

Colour reproduction by Colorscan
Printed in Great Britain

Design: Rod Teasdale
Airbrush Artwork: Chris Davey
Computer graphics: Richard Burgess

CONTENTS

INTRODUCTION

At some time or other, most readers have probably imagined themselves duelling with the 'Hun in the sun' during the Battle of Britain – at the controls of the legendary Spitfire. But what was the most famous fighter of the Second World War really like to fly and fight in?

Produced in greater numbers than any other British combat aircraft before or since the War–nearly 23,000 were built in 34 different variants (marks) – the Spitfire fought in every operational theatre and remained in front line service somewhere in the world for almost 20 years. And this was an aircraft originally designed to have a combat life of months rather than years.

Right: Reginald Joseph Mitchell, chief designer of the Supermarine Aviation Works designed a series of Schneider contest winning seaplanes – and the Spitfire.

The Spitfire became a legend in 1940 during the four month long Battle of Britain when it fought alongside the Hawker Hurricane to win a close-run victory over the hitherto undefeated *Luftwaffe*. It was the first occasion that a major battle had been won by air power alone. The Royal Air Force had retained air superiority over the British Isles. At the time credit for the victory was given to the young pilots who flew the fighters, named 'the few' by Prime Minister Winston Churchill in his famous speech to the House of Commons in August 1940.

Below: An RAF Supermarine Seagull III flying boat, developed from R J Mitchell's 1922 Schneider contest winner, the Sea Lion.

However, the foundations of the RAF's victory in the Battle of Britain were laid, not by the British government, but by six farsighted and talented individuals, without whom the Supermarine Spitfire would never have taken part in the crucial air battle. The six: Reginald Joseph Mitchell, Sir Henry Royce, Lady Houston, Hugh Dowding, Winston Churchill and Lord Beaverbrook all

contributed to the Spitfire legend.

Both its innovative airframe and superb engine were products of private enterprise and due to the financial depression of the 1930s, were almost cancelled by lack of funding.

The Supermarine Aviation Works Ltd was a small aircraft manufacturer based at Woolston on the banks of the River Itchen at Southhampton. Established in 1916 and specialising in the production of flying boats, a young draughtsman joined the company in the same year. His name –R J Mitchell. At the end of World War One, contracts were cancelled and to stimulate business, Mitchell

was tasked with designing a competitor for the Schneider Trophy, an international closed-course speed contest for maritime aircraft.

Against all the odds, Supermarine's biplane flying boat, the Sea Lion II, designed by Mitchell, won the 1922 Schneider contest at a speed of 145.72 mph. However, he would be best remembered for his innovative monoplane seaplane designs which won the contest in 1927. Mitchell rejected the high speed seaplane designs that had won the contest since 1919, choosing instead to build a compact monoplane with a metal fuselage. The resulting Supermarine S 4 had minimal funding from the Air Ministry and was

Above: Supermarine S 6B S1595, Mitchell's all-metal Rolls-Royce engined seaplane that won the Schneider Trophy outright for Great Britain in 1931.

Above: One of Mitchells's two Supermarine S.6Bs at Calshot that were victorious contenders for the 1931 Scheider Trophy contest.

Below: The prototype of the all-metal elliptical-winged Supermarine Spitfire fighter flew for the first time on 5 March 1936.

Mitchell's guidance. For his next Schneider design, Mitchell chose a Rolls-Royce engine in preference to the Napier powerplants used in the S 4/5. The S 6 would be an all-metal monoplane powered by a new lightweight 1,900hp Rolls-Royce 'R' (Racing) V12 engine which had to be designed and tested in six months if the aircraft was to take part in the 1929 contest. It was ready in time and the S 6 duly won the contest, held at Spithead in the Solent almost in sight of the Supermarine works. A few days later the same aircraft flown by Squadron Leader A H Orlebar raised the World Speed Record to 336.3 mph.

In 1931, the twelfth Schneider contest was held in Britain, again at Spithead. Mitchell's entry was the improved S 6B which featured larger floats and Rolls-Royce 'R' engine boosted to 2,300hp. However, the Air Ministry, under pressure from the then Labour government decided that due to the depression, it could not fund the RAF's High Speed Flight or the British entry in the contest.

The S 6, and thus the Spitfire, was saved by the intervention of 74-year-old Lady Houston. The wealthy widow of Sir Richard Houston, she sent a telegram to the Prime Minister Ramsey MacDonald saying, 'the supremacy of English airmen can only be upheld by their entry in the Schneider Trophy, and as I consider this of supreme importance, I will

operated by the RAF's High Speed Flight based at Calshot. On 13 September 1925, the S 4 broke the World Speed Record with a speed of 226.9 mph but crashed during final trials for that year's Schneider contest. However, in 1927, its more powerful successor, the S 5 finished in first and second places in the contest held at Venice.

The following year, when there was no Schneider contest, Supermarine was acquired by Vickers (Aviation) with a view to expanding the company's output under

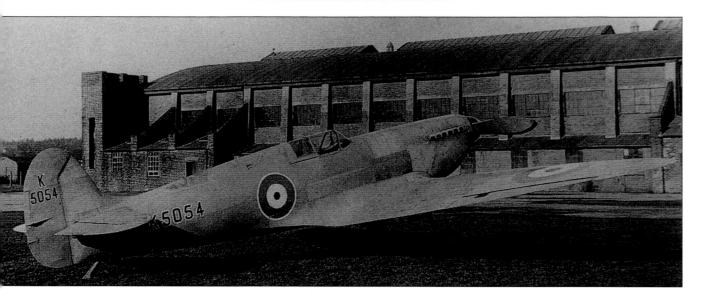

guarantee the whole amount of £100,000 that you consider necessary'. (That sum in today's terms is roughly equivalent to £6 million).

In the event, the French and Italian teams cried off at the last minute, so on 12 September 1931 the Schneider Trophy was won outright by Great Britain for all time by virtue of a third successive victory, when F/L J N Boothman completed the course at Spithead at a speed of 349.08 mph. To reinforce its victory, the same S 6B gained the World's Speed Record when F/Lt G H Stainforth recorded a speed of 407.5 mph, the seaplane becoming the first aircraft in the world to exceed 400 mph.

Encouraged by the success of the Rolls-Royce engined S 6B, Mitchell persuaded his company to try its hand at designing a modern front-line interceptor in response to Air Ministry Specification F7/30 issued at the

end of 1931. This was for a single-seat day and night fighter and resulted in Mitchell's Supermarine Type 224, a metal gull-winged monoplane with fixed undercarriage and an open cockpit powered by a 600 hp steam-cooled Rolls-Royce Goshawk which first flew on 20 February 1934. Although it was unofficially named the Spitfire, the Type 224 was a flop and the sole prototype scrapped.

In the meantime, Sir Henry Royce had authorised the development of a new V12 engine using technology gleaned from the 'R' engine. In early 1933, work began on the 1,000 hp PV. (Private Venture) 12 engine, although Royce died on 22 April, just as the final design drawings were completed. Nevertheless, the first PV.12 flew in a converted Hart biplane in April 1935 by which time, R J Mitchell had been given a free hand by his boss Sir Robert McLean to

Above: The unpainted prototype F37/34 parked outside of the Woolston works at Southampton. Note the original rudder shape.

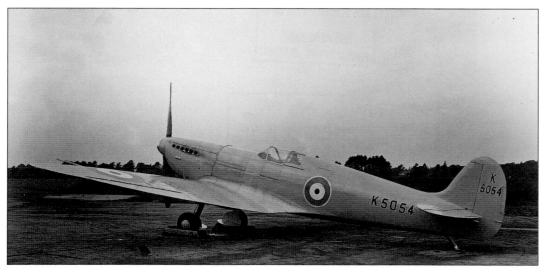

Left: Fitted with a new rudder and mainwheel doors, the Spitfire prototype K5054 was painted grey for the 1936 RAF Air Pageant at Hendon.

Above: Spitfire Mk 1 K9795 was delivered to 19 Sqn at Duxford in September 1939. It was damaged by anti-aircraft fire flying with 64 Sqn in the Battle of Britain.

design a state-of-the-art interceptor, far in advance of any existing Air Ministry specification. This time, the Supermarine Type 300, also christened the Spitfire, penned by Mitchell and his assistant Joseph Smith had become an all metal low-winged monoplane with a distinctive thin elliptical wing planform, fully retractable undercarriage and enclosed cockpit. Armed with no less than eight machine guns it was powered by a 990 hp production version of the Rolls-Royce PV.12, the Merlin.

So advanced was the new fighter that the Air Ministry re-wrote its specification to fit it

Right: Without the Rolls-Royce Merlin, which remained in production throughout the Second World War, there would have been no Spitfire or Hurricane.

Left: Vickers-Armstrong test pilot, Jeffrey Quill, flew the first prototype Spitfire on its second flight and later flew in the Battle of Britain with 65 Sqn.

and only weeks after its first flight on 5 March 1936, Supermarine was awarded a contract to produce 310 Spitfire Mk Is at a price of £7,500 each – less the 1,030hp Merlin II engine! This unexpected success caused consternation in the Woolston factory where the Supermarine production lines turned out small numbers of fabric and wire biplane flying boats, such as the Scapa and Walrus. With its stressed-skin metal fuselage and its very thin elliptical wing that had no straight parts in it, the Spitfire could not have been more different. Supermarine took almost two years to tool up for the job, even then the first Spitfires were virtually hand-built by craftsmen. It took up to three times as many man-hours to assemble each Spitfire compared to its future adversary, the German Messerschmitt Bf 109.

The first Spitfire Ia was delivered to the RAF in May 1938 by which time contracts for a further 1,200 aircraft had been placed. A series of modifications were introduced on the production lines. These included the replacement of the two-blade fixed-pitch wooden airscrew with a DH metal three-blade constant-speed prop, which added five

mph to its maximum speed, a 'bubble' canopy and a bullet-proof windscreen. Sadly, R J Mitchell never lived to see his creation in production. He died of cancer on 11 June 1937 at the age of 42, six months after the redoubtable Lady Houston, who passed away in December 1936. Three of the Spitfire's 'godparents' were gone, but three others would guide it through its baptism of fire during which time the legend was born.

Below: The 1030hp Rolls-Royce Merlin III V12 liquid-cooled engine developed from the PV.12, that powered the Spitfire Mk 1.

THREE WISE MEN

SIR HUGH C T DOWDING

Like Hermann Göring, the commander of the *Luftwaffe*, Hugh Dowding, had been a pilot during the First World War and had commanded squadrons of fighter aircraft in France. They had little else in common. A career officer with a single-minded determination to see the RAF given equal opportunities with its more senior service rivals, Dowding's set views and uncompromising stand on RAF issues denied him the rapid promotion some of his contemporaries enjoyed during the interwar years. However, he was appointed to the Air Council in 1931. With the rank of Air Marshal, as a Member of Supply and Research, he used his position to promote the latest advances of the day, such as monoplane fighter aircraft, which led to the Hurricane and Spitfire, and developing a system of fighter control using the latest radio and radar technology.

In 1936 Dowding became the first Commander-in-Chief of the newly created Fighter Command. It was regarded as a side-ways step by the Air Ministry, but the post gave him control of all of Britain's air defence assets: fighter aircraft, anti-aircraft guns and barrage balloons. He was already preparing for the Battle of Britain and the 1938 Munich crisis enabled him to acquire new support equipment for the RAF such as Sector Operation Rooms and paved runways at main fighter bases. He also oversaw the establishment of the Observer Corps, a volunteer organisation of sky watchers manned by ex-servicemen located throughout England to make visual reports of unidentified aircraft.

When war broke out, 58-year-old Dowding was putting the finishing touches to Britain's air defence network. The Spitfire force was still in the early stages of its creation, but it was already considered vital. During the Battle of France Dowding came into conflict with the new Prime Minister, Winston Churchill, when he refused to deploy any of his precious Spitfires to mainland France. In the event, Churchill accepted Dowding's decision and personally flew to France to inform the French government that RAF Spitfires were to be held back for the defence of Britain. While Dowding was considered by many of his pilots as withdrawn and aloof this view was softened somewhat when it was learnt that his son had just finished his course at RAF Cranwell and was about to be posted to 74 (Tiger) Squadron as a Flying Officer on the eve of the Battle of Britain – flying Spitfires.

WINSTON SPENCER CHURCHILL

From the very creation of the RAF in 1918, Winston Churchill, then Secretary of State for War and Air threw his weight behind Sir Hugh Trenchard's vigorous campaign to retain the service's independence. In the 1930s, as a backbench MP, Churchill spearheaded the re-armament faction in Parliament and was a severe critic of Prime Minister Neville Chamberlain's appeasement policy. At the outbreak of war, the 64-year-old Churchill was appointed First Lord of the Admiralty. On the day Germany invaded the Low Countries, 10 May 1940, Chamberlain resigned in favour of Winston Churchill who immediately put himself in the front line by undertaking a number of flights to France for last ditch efforts to prevent its government from capitulating. However, these missions failed to delay the inevitable and on 22 June France fell to Germany.

On 18 June Churchill had made a speech in the House of Commons warning that 'the Battle of France is over. I expect the Battle of Britain is about to begin'. Although he did not have a close personal relationship with Dowding, Churchill trusted him and left the task of defending Britain almost entirely to

Right: Air Marshal Sir Hugh Dowding oversaw the transition of Britain's air defence system from a ramshackle affair to the most modern in the world. The Commander-in-Chief of Fighter Command had the reputation as a dour individual, but his contribution to the British victory was enormous.

him during the summer of 1940. Churchill also became the first British Prime Minister to wear a uniform in office: that of the RAF. One of the most important and imaginative additions that Churchill made to his team of senior ministers on becoming Prime Minister was the establishment of a Ministry of Aircraft Production and giving it to the newspaper tycoon Lord Beaverbrook to run.

WILLIAM MAXWELL AITKIN, LORD BEAVERBROOK

A confirmed anglophile, the 61-year-old Canadian self-made millionaire owner of the *Daily Express* was an unlikely ally of Hugh Dowding, but they turned out to be an inspired team. Dowding had long been at loggerheads with the Air Staff and Beaverbrook, who had no patience with military red tape, virtually ignored it as he imposed mass production methods on Britain's aircraft factories.

Beaverbrook recruited top executives from the motor industry, research scientists from universities, established the Civil Repair Organisation (CRO) and persuaded many of his wealthy friends to contribute large sums of money to the 'Buy a Spitfire' fund and the public to give up their pots and pans to be turned into warplanes coining the phrase 'from the frying pan into the Spitfire'.

In April 1939 an order was placed for 1,000 Spitfires to be produced at a brand new 'shadow' factory at Castle Bromwich, the first deliveries of which were scheduled for January 1940. None had been delivered when Beaverbrook came into office but following his decision to replace the management and re-organise production practices, the first Castle Bromwich Spitfire Mk II, which featured a more powerful Merlin, took to the air on 6 June. It was followed by 125 more by the end of September. During the same period AA gun production was almost doubled, radar chains completed and Rolls-Royce increased production of Merlin engines at their Derby and Crewe factories to 400 a week. The output of the CRO, which was responsible for repairing battle damaged aircraft and returning them direct to operational units, also increased from 20 a week in June to 160 a week two months later.

Like Dowding, Beaverbrook had a personal stake in the battle. While he stampeded through the corridors of power, upsetting Civil Servants and Military 'Brass Hats' in the process, his only son, Squadron Leader the Honourable J W 'Max' Aitkin was leading 601 Sqn. During the opening weeks of the Battle of Britain he shot down eight German aircraft.

The real strength of Beaverbrook's relationship with Dowding was illustrated by the fact that the Minister phoned the Commander-in-Chief of Fighter Command on an almost daily basis to ask how the Battle was progressing and how he could be of help.

By ruthless red-tape cutting and simplification of production methods combined with charm and cunning, Beaverbrook succeeded in keeping replacements ahead of losses during the Battle of Britain. After the Battle was over, Dowding paid tribute the Canadian's contribution to its outcome by saying that 'the country owes as much to Beaverbrook for the Battle of Britain as it does to me'.

WARZONE
AIR DEFENCE BETWEEN THE WARS

At the end of the First World War, the newly independent Royal Air Force had a struggle to survive. Prime Minister Lloyd George announced that the days of the fledgling RAF as a separate department were numbered. He was opposed by Winston Churchill, then the Secretary of State for Air, who threw his weight behind the RAF's first Commander-in-Chief, Air Marshal Sir Hugh Trenchard and his campaign to retain the service's independence. Their campaign met with success when Parliament voted to accept Trenchard's proposals for the future organisation of an independent RAF at the end of 1919. It was a far reaching decision. However, the RAF budget for 1920 was limited to £15 million with provision for nineteen overseas squadrons but only six home squadrons plus two training wings.

In 1925 the Air Defence of Great Britain was placed under the control of Air Marshal Sir John Salmon. His command included the newly-created Auxiliary Air Force (AAF), the first squadrons of which were 602 (City of Glasgow) and 600 (City of London) Squadrons. Trenchard's aim was to make the part-time Auxiliary Air Force a prestigious elite by restricting membership to only the very best volunteers. Squadrons were formed as city or county –504 (County of Nottingham) or 603 (City of Edinburgh) –based units and soon gained the reputations of being the 'Best Clubs in Town'. The AAF also became an integral part of Great Britain's air defence and routinely took part in exercises with regular RAF squadrons. Its aircraft were part of the 700 that took part in the 'greatest air manoeuvres in history' defending Southeast England from 'foreign' invaders in August 1928.

Unfortunately, with economic decline threatening most of Europe, the RAF became an obvious target for cuts in government spending. In February 1932 the Rt Hon Arthur Henderson MP, leader of the Labour Party,

Right: RAF Bulldog biplane fighters, which comprised 70 per cent of Britain's fighter defences in the early 1930s, thrill crowds at the Hendon RAF Air Pageant.

opened the League of Nations Disarmament Conference in Geneva. Two months later, the Air Estimates reversed the previous five years' slow expansion, introducing a ten per cent cut in the budget. Once again, the long term future of the RAF was thrown into doubt. However, only a year later, Adolf Hitler came to power. Germany walked out of the League's Disarmament Conference and there were immediate calls by some Members of Parliament, including Winston Churchill, for Britain to re-arm without delay. At the time, Britain's air defences rested on thirteen RAF squadrons, the majority of which were equipped with outdated Bristol Bulldog biplanes.

The 1934 Air Estimates gave little indication of re-armament although the Prime Minister, Stanley Baldwin, assured the house that 'if the Disarmament Conference failed, steps would be taken to bring about an Air-Disarmament Convention; if that failed, the British Government would proceed to bring the strength of our Air Force up to the strength of the strongest air force within striking distance of this country'. Reassuring words! During the summer of 1934 the political situation in Europe deteriorated further. Baldwin's Disarmament Conference did fail and Germany resigned from the League of Nations. Fortunately, Britain's aircraft industry sensed the danger before the government,

and prepared for rapid expansion. The Air Ministry eventually issued new specifications for monoplane fighter aircraft, one of which was F7/30 that led indirectly to the birth of the Supermarine Spitfire.

By March 1935, the existence of Germany's *Luftwaffe* was officially revealed to the world. Astonishingly, it already possessed some 2,000 aircraft of all types manned by 20,000 officers and men. At that time, the RAF had 850 first-line aircraft, many of which were approaching obsolescence. In May the British Government announced proposals for further expansion of the RAF, envisaging a frontline strength of at least 1,500 aircraft by March 1937. Even these proposals looked

Above: The Hawker Hart family of two-seat fighters, light bombers and advanced trainers remained in service until the outbreak of World war Two.

Below: A Siskin IIIA fighter of 41 Sqn based at Northolt, a type which equipped eleven RAF home-based air defence squadrons up to 1932.

Above: A Gloster Gladiator Mk 1 wearing the colourful 1930s markings of 72 Sqn. The RAF's last biplane fighter fought in Norway, France and Britain and Malta.

inadequate later in the year. Germany re-introduced conscription, civil war raged in Austria and on 3 October, Italy invaded Abyssinia (Ethiopia). In March 1936 Hitler's forces moved into the Rhineland in violation of the Treaty of Versailles.

In response to these threatening developments, the Air Estimates for 1936-7 were almost twice as much as the previous year and made provisions for the establishment of 123 squadrons for the Home Defence Force. In the 1936 RAF Display held at Hendon on 27 June, the Supermarine Spitfire made its first public appearance. In the meantime, the international situation showed no sign of improving. Germany had formed an Axis with Italy and civil war had broken out in Spain involving pilots and aircraft from Germany's fledgling *Luftwaffe*.

In 1937, Winston Churchill, now a backbencher, was in the forefront of the re-armament faction in Parliament. He had already made his position clear, stating that 'the only real security upon which sound military principles will rely is that you should be master of your own air', and in the House

he deplored the London County Council's decision to ban local cadet corps and school children from attending the RAF Display dress rehearsal.

In August some 400 RAF aircraft were engaged in a mock attack on London which was defended by RAF interceptors and anti-aircraft guns. The interim phase of the RAF's expansion programme saw the introduction of Hawker Fury and Hart derivatives, the Gloster Gauntlet and the Gladiator –all biplanes –and diverse transport, training and communications types. These were to be followed by a new generation of monoplane bombers: the Battle, Blenheim and Wellington. But the most important of the new types that were awaited by the RAF were the Hurricane and Spitfire fighters.

By January 1938, the newly created Fighter Command, led by Air Chief Marshal Sir Hugh Dowding, possessed or was in the process of forming 26 Regular and Auxiliary fighter squadrons, only one of which, No 111 (F), had taken delivery of its first Hurricanes. Within days of the RAF's annual air defence exercises in August 1938, which involved

bombers from 'Eastland', an imaginary territory over the North Sea, all RAF leave was cancelled and Fighter Command was bought to an operational state of readiness. The Munich Crisis had begun.

Auxiliary Air Force squadrons were deployed to their war stations and their aircraft's silver paint schemes and colourful squadron markings replaced by unfamiliar drab camouflage. The RAF's first operational Spitfire Squadron, No 19, had just been formed. To prevent the crisis escalating into another major war, the British Prime Minister Neville Chamberlain asked for a summit meeting with the German Chancellor, Adolf Hitler, and flew to Germany on 29 September 1938. Chamberlain returned the following day having signed the Munich Agreement which allowed Hitler to seize the Czechoslovak frontier region of Sudetenland. The Agreement, condemned by Churchill as appeasement, nevertheless held Europe back from all-out war, while the crisis gave added impetus to the RAF and AAF expansion programmes.

It did not, however, curb Hitler's appetite for enlarging his 'empire'. In March 1939, Bohemia-Moravia and Memel were annexed. German troops entered Prague. On 28 March, Madrid fell to General Franco's forces supported by Heinkel He 111 bombers and Messerschmitt Bf109 fighters of the German Condor Legion. Three days later the British Government abandoned its appeasement policy and announced that it would guarantee the sovereignty of Poland against any attack from Germany.

There was now no turning back. War was now all but inevitable.

Deliveries of the new RAF fighter types increased. The first Auxiliary Air Force Squadron, 602 (City of Glasgow) replaced its Gauntlet biplanes with Spitfires in May 1938. Large scale air defence exercises in which 1,300 RAF aircraft and 53,000 personnel participated were held over several days in August and at the end of the month Royal Air Force and RAF reservists were mobilized.

On 1 September Operation *Weiss* began when Hitler's forces invaded Poland and two days later, Britain declared war on Germany. World War II had begun.

Above: Having entered service in 1932, the Tiger Moth remained the RAF's most widely used elementary trainer throughout World War Two.

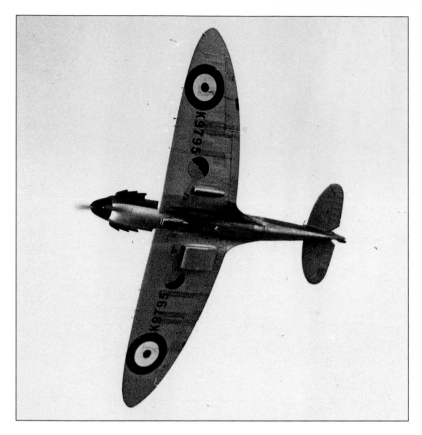

SPITFIRE AT WAR

At the outbreak of the war the *Luftwaffe* claimed to have more than 4,000 aircraft of all types in service while the RAF had 3,555 aircraft of all types on strength and 20,033 aircrew. Britain's main fighter defences were still manned by more than 500 biplanes although 347 Hurricanes equipped a total of 16 squadrons. Of the 270 Spitfire Mk.1s delivered to the RAF at the time, 187 had been issued to nine operational squadrons while two others were in the process of re-equipping.

Above: The 9th production Spitfire Mk I showing off its elliptical wing, was delivered to 19 Sqn September 1939 and fought in the Battle of Britain with 64 and 603 Sqns.

It was only three days into the war when RAF Spitfires and Hurricanes fired their guns in anger – but with tragic results. On 6 September, a flight of unidentified aircraft were reported to have crossed the Essex coast heading for London. As a precautionary measure, the North Weald Sector Controller scrambled a flight of six 56 Sqn Hurricanes from North Weald airfield. However, the Squadron CO decided to order all of his serviceable aircraft, fourteen of them, into the air. Responding to reports of more aircraft in the air from jittery Observer Corps, six more Hurricanes from 151 Sqn were scrambled. Once this force of 20 aircraft failed to find any 'bandits' they turned inland heading east and were fired on by 'trigger happy' anti-

aircraft guns. This in turn led to 24 Spitfires from 54, 65 and 74 Sqns at Hornchurch being scrambled. Guided towards the 'enemy' aircraft by the anti-aircraft fire, the Spitfires shot down two of 56 Sqn's Hurricanes. One pilot was killed. Air raid sirens sounded throughout east London and Essex and yet more Spitfires, this time from 19 and 66 Sqns at Duxford, were scrambled to join the confusion. At the last minute, the commanding officer of 151 Sqn realised that the sky was full of RAF fighters attacking each other and managed to warn those in the air and on the ground to call off the action over his R/T. Unfortunately the 'ack-ack' (anti-aircraft) batteries at Sheerness and Chelmsford did not get the message in time and fired on the Spitfires returning to Hornchurch, damaging at least one. This unfortunate 'accident of war' became known as the 'Battle of Barking Creek'.

Thankfully, the next occasion in which RAF Spitfires went into combat it was not an all-British battle. On 16 October, Junkers Ju 88 bombers of KG.30 based at Westerland attacked Royal Navy facilities in the Firth of Forth. They were intercepted by Spitfires of 602 (City of Glasgow) –the very first AAF unit to be formed and the first to re-equip with the type –and 603 (City of Edinburgh) Sqns from RAF Turnhouse. Two Ju 88s were shot down during the encounter while 603 Sqn shot down a Heinkel He 111 of KG.26 in a separate raid. Five weeks later these two AAF squadrons were responsible for bringing down the first *Luftwaffe* aircraft on the British mainland when they shot down another KG.26 He 111 over Lothian on 29 November.

Meanwhile on mainland Europe, Germany's invasion and defeat of Poland was followed by a lull in the fighting, a period known as 'Phoney War' which lasted until April 1940 when Germany invaded Denmark and Norway. RAF bombers, supported by RAF Hurricanes and Gladiators and Fleet Air Arm Sea Gladiators and Skuas were despatched to Norway, but it was too little, too late. The surviving Hurricanes and Gladiators were lost when the aircraft carrier *Glorious* was intercepted and sunk by two German battlecruisers.

On 10 May, Operation *Gelb*, the German offensive against France and the Low Countries began. On the same day, Neville Chamberlain resigned as Prime Minister in favour of Winston Churchill. His coalition government included Sir Archibald Sinclair as Secretary of State for Air, and Lord Beaverbrook as head of the newly created

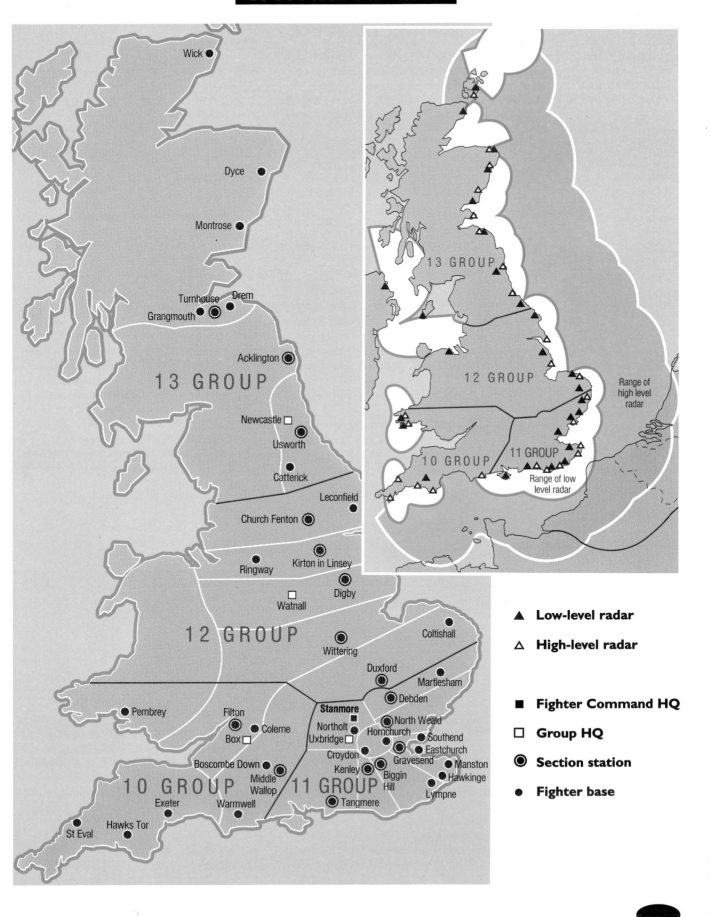

Wick

Dyce

Montrose

Turnhouse   Drem
Grangmouth

Acklington

13 GROUP

Newcastle ☐
Usworth

Catterick

Leconfield

Church Fenton

Ringway   Kirton in Linsey

Digby
Watnall ☐

12 GROUP

Coltishall

Wittering

Duxford
Martlesham

Debden

Pembrey

Filton
Colerne   **Stanmore**
Box ☐   Northolt   North Weald
             Uxbridge ☐ Hornchurch
                         Southend
             Croydon   Eastchurch
Boscombe Down   Gravesend
             Kenley   Manston
Middle   Biggin   Hawkinge
Wallop   **11 GROUP**   Hill
10 GROUP   Lympne
Exeter   Warmwell   Tangmere
Hawks Tor
St Eval

13 GROUP

12 GROUP

Range of
high level
radar

10 GROUP   **11 GROUP**

Range of low
level radar

▲ **Low-level radar**

△ **High-level radar**

■ **Fighter Command HQ**

☐ **Group HQ**

◉ **Section station**

● **Fighter base**

Right: A Spitfire Mk I of 66 Sqn, the second unit to be equipped with the new fighter in 1938. Note the wooden two-blade fixed-pitch propellor.

Below: Spitfire Mk Is of 65 Sqn in April 1939 fitted with three-blade variable-pitch airscrews. K9906 in the lead is flown by Battle of Britain ace 'Bob' Tuck.

Ministry of Aircraft Production. Three days later, RAF Spitfires of 66 Sqn tangled with Bf 109s escorting Ju 87 Stukas, claiming to have downed a number of the *Luftwaffe* aircraft for the loss of one of their own.

The following day, 74 Sqn Spitfires flew cover over a destroyer bringing the Dutch royal family to Britain. Holland had capitulated. Operating from bases in France, the British Expeditionary Force's Air Component consisted mainly of Battle and Blenheim light bombers of the Advanced Air Striking Force (AASF) supported by Hurricane fighters. Despite repeated pleas from the

French government, Sir Hugh Dowding refused to commit any Fighter Command Spitfires to the Battle of France. On 16 May Churchill flew to France, ironically escorted by RAF Spitfires of 92 Sqn, to inform the French government that Britain could spare no more fighters for the defence of France. The brunt of the aerial fighting there was borne by 261 RAF Hurricanes drawn from five squadrons, only 66 of which were to return to England.

However, Spitfires did see action over France in May and June 1940. On 23 May, Spitfires of 74 and 92 Sqns operating from

Hornchurch met the Messerschmitt Bf 109 in combat for the first time, resulting in the loss of four Spitfires, one of which was captured intact after a forced landing at Calais; the squadrons claimed to have destroyed six Bf 109s in the encounter. A single Spitfire of 212 Sqn, a detachment of RAF's Special Survey Flight, had been based in France since November 1939. This was a specially modified photo reconnaissance aircraft which provided valuable intelligence for the BEF as the situation in France deteriorated and German units closed up to the coastline. It continued its covert operations until the fall of France.

Following the surrender of the Belgium

Above: On the eve of the War, 12 Group Spitfire Mk 1s of 611 Sqn exercise over their base at Digby. Note the close 'vic' formation over the airfield.

Left: The KG.26 He 111 shot down by Spitfire Is of 602 and 603 (City of Edinburgh) Sqns on 29 November, the first bought down on the British mainland. Note the 'double crosses' on the wings.

army on 25 May and the fall of Calais and Boulogne two days later, the British War cabinet issued the order to activate Operation *Dynamo* –the seaborne evacuation of the British Expeditionary Force from Dunkirk, the only North Sea port still in Allied hands. British fighter cover for the operation which began on 26 May was to be provided by 16 Fighter Command squadrons drawn from the 32 units from all over Great Britain.

The nine day evacuation of 338,226 men from the beaches of Dunkirk was carried out despite air raids by *Luftwaffe* bombers. The Hurricanes and Spitfires, air defence fighters built for speed and agility, had small fuel tanks and thus limited range. The Spitfire could fight for only a few minutes over Dunkirk before breaking for home to refuel. Nevertheless, the RAF flew 2,739 fighter sorties and lost 406 fighters –69 of them Spitfires.

On June 12, two days after Italy declared war on Great Britain and France, Churchill flew to Tours in a last vain effort to convince the French not to give up. It was only the low fuel state of his escorting Spitfires made him leave with his mission unaccomplished. The

following day Paris was declared an open city. The Germans marched in and on 21 June France signed an armistice with Germany. The Battle of France was over and Britain faced its own battle for survival.

Above: A 602 (City of Glasgow) Sqn pilot adjusts his helmet before climbing into his Spitfire I.

'THE FEW'
FLYING TRAINING

The Battle of Britain was won by the quality of the RAF's pilots as much as the quality of the aircraft that they flew. At the outbreak of war, pilots for the new interceptor were drawn from a variety of backgrounds, Royal Air Force Regulars, Auxiliary Air Force 'club' members, RAF Volunteer Reservists –spare time flyers, and University Air Squadrons –student volunteers. It was said at the time that 'Auxiliaries are gentlemen trying to be officers, Regulars are officers trying to be gentlemen and VRs are neither trying to be both'.

Regulars had passed through the RAF College at Cranwell where they were given basic and advanced training on biplane types before being commissioned as officers and posted to fighter or Army Co-operative squadrons. In the late 1930s these were equipped with Hawker Fury IIs and Hinds, or Gloster Gauntlets –all fabric and wire biplanes.

Auxiliary pilots were educated, intelligent and good pilots who adapted well to metal monoplanes when they came into service. All commissioned officers, they tended to be up to five years older than their Regular counterparts. Most were men of independent means.

RAFVR pilots were enthusiasts who sacrificed much of their spare time to maintain the high standards demanded of them. Their flying training was paid for by the government and, on gaining their wings, they became sergeant pilots.

By the mid-1930s, most RAF pilots, irrespective of their method of entry, were being given their basic training on the DH Tiger Moth. The two-seat biplane primary trainer entered service with RAF Elementary and Reserve Flying Schools in 1932 replacing First World War-vintage Avro 504s, and was destined to remain in service for more than 20 years. After some 50 hours on the Tiger Moth, trainee fighter pilots graduated to the two-seat Hart trainer, another biplane also introduced in 1932. However, the Hart's top speed was only 165 mph which hardly prepared a student pilot for the new generation of 350 mph monoplane fighters about to enter service.

To address this problem new monoplane training types were also ordered –the Miles Magister or 'Maggie' elementary trainer and the Miles Master advanced trainer which had retractable undercarriage, an enclosed cockpit and a top speed of 225 mph.

However, few of these new trainers were in service when war broke out and in an attempt to plug the short-fall, 400 North American Harvard advanced trainers were ordered, the first of which were delivered to RAF Flying Training Schools (FTS) in early 1939. This popular and robust trainer would remain in RAF service until the mid-1950s. One problem was converting RAF instructors to these new types before *ab initio* students

could get their hands on them. Consequently, many pilots took part in the Battle of Britain having been taught to fly on obsolete biplane trainers, with little R/T or tactics training.

Both Regulars and Auxiliaries practised set piece air battle scenarios based on First World War tactics right up to 1939. At the beginning of the Second World War the RAF was getting 200 pilots a month from flying training of all types, but they were taught by instructors with no operational experience and many of them had never flown a monoplane or used a radio. Operational training flights concentrated on tight formation flying and 'Fighting Area Attacks' in which a line of fighters queued up to take turns to fire at a target aircraft. There were also few opportunities of firing guns at a moving target.

The first impressions of flying the Spitfire by pilots who fought in the Battle Britain vary. Douglas Bader, who had lost both his legs in a pre-war flying accident, fought most of the Battle of Britain leading a Hurricane squadron but began the war flying Spitfires. Paul Brickhill describes his first impression of a 19 Sqn 'Spit' in early 1940: 'It would be all right as soon as he got into a Spitfire, but in the morning the pilots flew off to do convoy

patrols from an advanced base and no serviceable Spitfire was left. He flew a Magister instead. The same thing happened next day. Then the next morning he climbed into a Spitfire and a boy of twenty showed him the cockpit. Above the throttle quadrant were the switches of a TR.2 radio set. Bader had not used radio in the air yet. The boy rattled on about R/T procedure, making it sound so complicated that Bader impatiently cut him short and said he'd do without it this trip –just concentrate on the flying. She started easily and he took off without any nerves, feeling instantly that she was extremely sensitive fore and aft.

'The long, mullet-head cowling that housed the Merlin engine made for restricted vision, but he rapidly got the feel of her and liked the way she handled like a highly-strung thoroughbred. On the downwind leg he started his drill for landing and found he could not move the undercart selector lever into the 'down' position. No tugs, pushes or fiddlings would budge it. Disconcerting! Only one thing to do –'ring up' and get advice. He switched on the radio and like many of the ill-tuned early models it crackled and popped and buzzed, so that he could not hear a word

Above: Known as 'Maggie', the Miles Magister was the first low-wing monoplane trainer to be adopted by RAF Elementary Flying Training Schools in 1938.

Far Left: Most RAF Spitfire pilots flew their first solo flights in the DH Tiger Moth, more than 1,000 of which had been delivered by the outbreak of War.

Above: With an enclosed cockpit, retractable undercarriage and top speed of 205mph, the Harvard advanced trainer was the nearest thing to a two-seat Spitfire.

from the control tower. That was more disconcerting! He tried with the undercart selector lever again and after some time fiddling with this and the pump handle finally got things working and the two green lights winked reassuringly as the wheels locked down. After that the landing was an anti-climax, but neat.

'Old emotions were stirring. In this elite of beardless youth he had more seniority than anyone, twice as many flying hours as most and was years older. Long ago he had been the golden boy of such a squadron and now he was the new boy –the 'sprog'. Like a tide in him now rose the need to prove himself equal to the young pilots who could play rugger and wore their uniforms with such blithe assurance. Not for a moment did he admit there was anything he could not do as well as they (apart from rugger, which he accepted), but there are other impulses in the mind than those of the conscious.

'The old challenge. A new struggle'[1].

Douglas Bader scored 22 kills before his Spitfire collided with a Bf 109 over France in 1943 and he parachuted into captivity.

Alan Christopher 'Al' Deere sailed from his native New Zealand in 1937 to join the RAF as a Regular Officer, shot down 14 German aircraft during the Battles of France and Britain flying Spitfires with 54 Sqn, and was himself shot down nine times in the process. He describes his first flight in a Spitfire at Hornchurch: 'On 6 March 1939, I flew my first Spitfire, an aircraft very little different from the later Marks with which the RAF finished the war. In many respects, however, it was a nicer aircraft and certainly much lighter than subsequent Marks which became over-powered and over-weighted with armour plating and cannons.

'The transition from slow biplanes to the faster monoplanes was effected without fuss, and in a matter of weeks we were nearly as competent on Spitfires as we had been on Gladiators. When one hundred percent established with Spitfires, 54 Sqn flew its Gladiators up to Turnhouse to be handed over to 603 Auxiliary Sqn, the weekenders from Edinburgh. On the way up the squadron landed at Driffield to refuel and I was able to meet up again with two friends who had come over from New Zealand with me and it was good to hear that they, too, had never for one single moment regretted the decision to join the Royal Air Force.

'Two days after my first flight in a Spitfire, I was sent down to Eastleigh airfield near Southampton to collect a new aircraft from the Supermarine Works where the Spitfire was produced. The weather was pretty bad for the trip and I had the greatest difficulty finding Hornchurch. Such was my relief when I did find the airfield that I couldn't resist a quick beat-up, very much frowned on in those days. I noticed as I taxied towards the squadron hangar after landing that there was more than the normal complement of pilots to greet me.

I was soon to learn why. Not only had I committed the sin of beating up the airfield, I had neglected to change from fine to coarse pitch after take-off from Eastleigh with the result that there was a great deal more noise than normal on my quite small beat-up and, worse still, the brand new Spitfire was smothered in oil thrown out by the over-revving engine. A very red-faced Pilot Officer faced an irate 'Bubbles' Love, my flight commander, who was decent enough to let the matter rest at a good 'ticking-off'.

'Training on Spitfires followed the same pattern as on Gladiators, except that we did a little more cine-gun work to get practice on the new reflector sight with which the aircraft was fitted.

'One unsatisfactory piece of equipment was the small transmitter which emitted a regular squadron identification signal (IFF) to enable Operations to fix the position of aircraft. Unfortunately whenever the instrument (known to pilots as 'Pip-Squeak') was transmitting its signal, the pilot was unable to hear or be heard, and thus he missed many messages. Also the transmitters tended to get out of phase and aircraft were often wrongly identified as a result. This shortcoming was demonstrated on one famous occasion when a flight from 74 Sqn, led by F/L Paddy Treacy, was being homed on fixes taken from the transmission of a 54 Sqn aircraft. Finally, Paddy when out of R/T range and short of fuel, let down below cloud to find himself over France where his flight force-landed, with a certain amount of damage to aircraft. Voice fixing, whereby the pilot merely pressed his R/T switch for a short period, eventually replaced this most unreliable system.'[2]

'Al' Deere finished the war as a Wing Commander with 22 kills, 10 'probables' and 18 'damaged'.

H R 'Dizzy' Allen was compelled to apply for a commission in the RAF after seeing a Spitfire in flight in 1938. When he was posted to an operational Spitfire squadron, No 66 at Duxford in 1940, he had 145 solo flying

Below: The basic instrument panel of the 'string and fabric' Tiger Moth trainer is clearly seen in the instructor's rear cockpit.

Above: A pupil struggles into the rear cockpit of a North American Harvard I wearing his bulky parachute at an RAF Flying Training School in July 1940.

hours in his logbook –but had never flown a Spitfire! Here he records his first flight: 'At 8 a.m. on the dot the next day I reported to my new Flight Commander F/L Billy Bragg. His office was contained in a tent, he had an adequate enough desk, a locker for his flying clothing and little else. I saluted smartly and called him 'sir'. His return of my obeisance was to nod his head in acknowledgement. He was small, tough, with excellent manners, erect, a product of the RAF College at Cranwell but rather dull –he smoked a pipe. We chatted about this and that while he was reading my pilot's logbook to see what experience of the air I had gained, and he then came to his decision.

'*Flight Sergeant*' he bawled.

'A head poked round the flap of the tent, a Flight Sergeant materialised, marched to the desk, saluted, remained strictly at attention and replied:

'*Sir*!'

'At ease, Flight. This is our newly joined pilot.'

'Flight Sergeant Dennis relaxed, turned to me and I shook him by the hand. He gave me a salute in return even though I was only an acting Pilot Officer.

'Flight,' Bragg said, 'could you drag out our oldest Spitfire for this new officer to make his first solo flight? What about LZ-X? Isn't that

the one in need of a major overhaul in a few more flying hours?'

'That's right, sir,' Dennis replied, 'She's almost in need of a 250 hour inspection.'

'How fortuitous,' Bragg said. 'Even if he does prang it won't matter too much. Get it ready if you would.'

Dennis saluted, gave me a grin and left.

'Anything you want to know about flying the Spitfire?' Bragg inquired.

'Not really,' I replied. 'In this business I reckon one has to find out for oneself.'

'I went to the locker room, climbed into my flying kit, shoved the parachute on to my shoulder and staggered out to LZ-X. Billy Bragg was there waiting for me. I strapped the parachute on, scrambled on to the wing and the rigger helped me into the cockpit. Billy climbed on to the wing and gave me the cockpit drill; there were, of course, no dual control Spitfires in those days, so one's first solo flight in these aircraft was similar to one's first ever solo in a Tiger Moth. Before he jumped off the wing, Billy gave me his final words of advice.

'Keep it clearly in mind that she is extremely sensitive fore and aft.'

'The Rolls-Royce Merlin engine developed over 1,000 horsepower, and I eased the throttle open gingerly on the grass airfield. As I tentatively gave her full boost, I felt the great

tug of the torque and had to wrestle with the aircraft to regain control. This aircraft was a Mark I model with a three bladed propeller, whereas the prototype had only two blades. The torque on the prototype must have been almost beyond the average man's strength to control. At this stage, one could only put the airscrew into fine pitch for take-off and landing, and coarse pitch for normal cruising. One was in bottom gear so to speak for take-off, and top gear for normal flight. Later, after suitable modifications, it was possible to control the pitch of the propeller through the whole spectrum.

'LZ-X lurched over the rough field gaining speed and I eased the stick forward only to be horrified by the immediate reaction which almost caused the propeller to dig into the grass. I over-corrected and she almost fell back on to her tail wheel. Billy was quite right; she was extremely sensitive fore and aft. However, we bumped into the air and I put her into a climb. Then I had to retract the undercarriage. This was achieved on the early models by pumping with a large black lever which required about thirty vigorous pulls and pushes to do the job. I pushed and pulled on the lever until I saw the green warning lights vanish and red lights appear, meaning the undercart was fully up.

'Meanwhile due to my exertions the Spitfire had nosed up and down in a dangerous manner as she commenced to climb, because my muscular efforts with the right arm had affected my left hand which held the control column. I climbed, making sure my oxygen system was functioning properly, until I was at thirty thousand feet. LZ-X might well have been ready for a major maintenance inspection but to me she was my personal swallow. I rolled, I dived, I came up on the zoom and stall-turned her. She was as light as a feather on the controls, almost dangerously so. I put her into a dive and watched with satisfaction the air speed indicator build up to something over four hundred mph, much the fastest speed I had then ever achieved.

'I have no words worthy of describing the Spitfire; it was an aircraft quite out of this world. There was certainly no love/hate relationship between me and my Spitfire; there was only love on my account, and on not one occasion did any of these aircraft let me down. I suffered quite grievous injuries when flying Spitfires, but they were due to my own errors or other factors, certainly not because of any fault in the design of the aircraft. I bounced on landing, but not all that badly. Certainly not badly enough to have to report a heavy landing so that checks should be made by the ground crew.'[1]

'Dizzy' Allen also survived the war with the

Above: A well-worn Spitfire Ia belonging to the Operational Training Unit at RAF Hawarden where most Battle of Britain pilots had their first Spitfire flight.

rank of Wing Commander and a score of at least 10 aircraft destroyed'.

Richard Hillary was at Oxford University when war broke out and had learned to fly with University Air Squadron. He immediately reported to the RAF Volunteer Reserve Centre and waited to be drafted to an initial training wing. Six months later he was posted to an Operational Training Unit (OTU) for a Spitfire conversion course: 'We learned the importance of getting to know our ground crews and to appreciate their part in a successful day's fighting, to make a careful check-up before taking off, but not to be hypercritical, for the crews would detest and resent any lack of confidence at once.

'And we learned, finally, to fly the Spitfire.

'I faced the prospect with some trepidation. Here for the first time was a machine in which there was no chance of making a dual circuit as a preliminary. I must solo right off, and in the fastest machine in the world.

'One of the squadron took me up for a couple of trips in a Miles Master, the British trainer most similar to a Spitfire in characteristics. I was put through half an hour's instrument flying under the hood in a Harvard, and then I was ready. At least I hoped I was ready. Kilmartin, a slight dark-haired Irishman in charge of our Flight, said: 'Get your parachute and climb in. I'll just show you the cockpit before you go off.'

'He sauntered over to the machine, and I found myself memorising every detail of his appearance with the clearness of a condemned man on his way to the scaffold –the chin sunk into the folds of a polo sweater, the leather pads on the elbows, and the string-darned hole in the seat of the pants. He caught my look of anxiety and grinned.

'Don't worry; you'll be surprised how easy she is to handle.'

'I hoped so.

'The Spitfires stood in two lines outside 'A' Flight pilots' room. The dull grey-brown of the camouflage could not conceal the clear-cut beauty, the wicked simplicity of their lines. I hooked up my parachute and climbed awkwardly into the low cockpit. I noticed how small was my field of vision. Kilmartin swung himself on to a wing and started to run through the instruments. I was conscious of his voice, but heard nothing of what he said. I was to fly a Spitfire. It was what I had most wanted through all the long dreary months of training. If I could fly a Spitfire, it would be worth it. Well, I was about to achieve my ambition and felt nothing. I was numb, neither exhilarated nor scared. I noticed the white enamel undercarriage handle. 'Like a lavatory plug,' I thought.

'What did you say?'

Kilmartin was looking at me and I realised I had spoken aloud. I pulled myself together.

'Have you got all that?' he asked.

'Yes, sir.'

'Well, off you go then. About four circuits and bumps. Good luck!'

'He climbed down.

'I taxied slowly across the field,

Left: The pilot's forward view when taxying a Spitfire on the ground is severely obsured by its long nose so he has to zig-zag his way across the airfield.

Below: After a take-off run of only 300 yards, the pilot of this OTU Spitfire has to remember to retract the undercarriage before closing the canopy.

remembering suddenly what I had been told; that the Spitfire's prop was long and that it was therefore inadvisable to push the stick too far forward when taking off; that the Spitfire was not a Lysander and that any hard application of the brake when landing would result in a somersault and immediate transfer to a Battle squadron. Because of the Battle's lack of power and small armament this was regarded by everyone as the ultimate disgrace.

'I ran quickly through my cockpit drill, swung the nose into wind, and took off. I had been flying automatically for several minutes before it dawned on me that I was actually in the air, undercarriage retracted and half-way round the circuit without incident. I turned into wind and hauled up on my seat, at the same time pushing back the hood. I came in low, cut the engine just over the boundary hedge, and floated down on all three points. I took off again. Three more times I came round for a perfect landing. It was too easy. I waited across wind for a minute and watched with

satisfaction several machines bounce badly as they came in. Then I taxied rapidly back to the hangars and climbed out nonchalantly. Noel, who had not yet soloed, met me.

'How was it?' he said.

I made a circle of approval with my thumb and forefinger.

'Money for old rope,' I said.

'I didn't make another good landing for a week.

'The flight immediately following our first solo was an hour's aerobatics. I climbed up to 12,000 feet before attempting even a slow roll. Kilmartin had said 'See if you can make her talk.' That meant the whole bag of tricks, and I wanted ample room for mistakes and possible blacking-out. With one or two very sharp movements on the stick I blacked myself out for a few seconds, but the machine was sweeter to handle than any other that I had flown. I put it through every manoeuvre that I knew of and it responded beautifully. I ended with two flick rolls and turned back for

Above: An OTU Spitfire on finals at 75-85mph with canopy open, flaps fully extended and Merlin throttled back to idle.

home. I was filled with a sudden exhilarating confidence. I could fly a Spitfire; in any position I was its master. It remained to be seen whether I could fight in one.

'We also had to put in an oxygen climb to 28,000 feet, an air-firing exercise, formation attacks, and numerous dog fights. The oxygen climb was uneventful but lengthy. It was interesting to see what a distance one ended up from the aerodrome even though climbing all the way in wide circles. Helmet, goggles, and oxygen mask gave me a feeling of restriction, and from then on I always flew with my goggles up, except when landing. The results of this were to be far-reaching.

'The air-firing exercise was uneventful, but as short as the oxygen climb had been long. We were given a few rounds in each gun and sent off to fire them into the Severn. All eight guns roared out from a quick pressure on the fire button on the control stick. The noise through the enclosed cabin was muffled, but the round caused a momentary drop in speed of forty miles per hour'.[4]

Richard Hillary joined 603 (City of Edinburgh) Sqn and scored two kills during the Battle of Britain before being shot down and severely burned. He wrote of his experiences in the classic book *The Last Enemy* but was killed on a night training flight in 1943.

James Edgar 'Johnnie' Johnson tried to join the Auxiliary Air Force in 1938 but was rejected. On the outbreak of war he joined the RAF Volunteer Reserve and first flew a Spitfire at the Harwarden OTU: 'The day I flew a Spitfire for the first time was one to remember. To begin with the instructor walked me round the lean fighter plane, drab in its war coat of brown and green camouflage paint, and explained the flight-

Far right: During the first months of the war, Spitfire pilots were continued to be taught to fly close 'vic' formations which proved to be disastrous in combat.

control system. Afterwards I climbed into the cockpit while he stood on the wing root and explained the functions of the various controls. I was oppressed by the narrow cockpit for I am reasonably wide across the shoulders and when I sat on the parachute each forearm rubbed uncomfortably on the metal sides.

'Bit tight across the shoulders for me?' I inquired.

'You'll soon get used to it,' he replied. 'Surprising how small you can get when one of those yellow-nosed brutes is on your tail. You'll keep your head down then! And get a stiff neck from looking behind. Otherwise you won't last long!' —and with this boost to my morale we pressed on with the lesson. After a further half-hour spent memorising the various emergency procedures and the handling characteristics, the instructor checked my harness straps and watched while I adjusted the leather flying-helmet.

'Start her up!'

'I carried out the correct drill and the Merlin sprang into life with its usual song of power, a sound no fighter pilot will easily forget. The instructor bellowed into my ear; 'You're trimmed for take-off. Don't forget your fine pitch, otherwise you'll never get off the ground. Good luck.' And he ambled away with a nonchalant air, but I knew that he would watch my take-off and landing with critical eyes.

'I trundled awkwardly over the grass surface swinging the Spitfire from side to side with brakes and bursts of throttle. This business was very necessary for the long, high nose of the aircraft made direct forward vision impossible and more than one pupil had recently collided with other Spitfires or petrol bowsers. I reached the very edge of the airfield, and before turning into wind carried out a final cockpit check. No aircraft was in sight on the circuit and I had the whole airfield to myself. I swung her nose into the wind. No more delays now, get off. Throttle gently but firmly open to about four pounds of boost. She accelerates very quickly, much faster than the Master. Stick forward to lift the tail and get a good airflow over the elevators. Correct a tendency to swing with coarse rudder. No more bouncing about. We can't be airborne yet! Yes, we are, and already climbing into the sky. Things move fast in the Spitfire! Wheels up. Pitch control back and throttle set to give a climbing speed of 200 mph. Close the hood. After a struggle, during which the nose rose and fell like the flight of a magpie, I closed the perspex canopy and

the cockpit seemed even more restricted than before. I toyed with the idea of flying with the hood open, but I could not fly or fight at high altitudes in this fashion and I must get acquainted with every feature of the plane.

Now it was time to take a firm hand with this little thoroughbred, for so far she had been the dominant partner in our enterprise. I carried out an easy turn and tried to pick up my bearings. Not more than twenty miles from Hawarden. I flew back, gaining confidence with every second. A Master looms ahead and slightly below. I overtake him comfortably, and to demonstrate my superiority attempt an upward roll. I forget to allow for the heavy nose of the Spitfire with sufficient forward movement of the stick and we barrel out of the manoeuvre, losing an undignified amount of height. Better concentrate on the handling characteristics and leave the aerobatics for another day. Over Hawarden again. Throttle back to a circuit speed. Hood open. All clear ahead. Wheels down and curve her across wind. Now the flaps and a final turn into wind. 120 mph on the approach and we are too high. Throttle back and she drops like a stone. 100 mph and over the boundary. Stick back and head over the side to judge the landing. Too high and in a semi-stalled condition we drop out of the sky to hit the unyielding ground with a hefty smack. As I suspected, my instructor had seen it all and was there when I switched off the engine.

'I saw the Spit get you into the air! And given a fair chance she would have carried out a better landing than yours! If you make a mess of your approach, open up and go round again. You've been told that with every plane you've flown. Get into the front seat of that Master and I'll show you a Spitfire circuit.'

'To be relegated back to the second team, as it were, was a severe jolt to my pride.

'Right, I've got her, Johnson. We're on the down-wind leg. The Spit is heavier than the Master and soon loses height when you cut the power. So make your circuit tight and try to get a steady, continuous turn from here. It looks good. You're down quickly, and if you're turning you can watch the sky behind. Remember that when you're down south, for you're a sitting duck on the circuit! Wheels down and adjust the trim. Flaps down. Continue the turn. Now into wind. Plenty of height –perhaps a little too much so we side-slip a bit off –so! Throttle right back. Ease back the stick and check her. She's sinking. Stick right back and she's down. Piece of cake, isn't it?'

manoeuvre which would cause my artificial horizon to topple, and burned off some of the 100 octane fuel in the tanks of the Spitfire to ease the problem of landing.

'Then I slowly lost height, joined the airfield circuit –there was no R/T communication between me and the ground –worked out in what direction I should attempt to land by the direction indicated by a paraffin-lit arrow, flew downwind in the circuit and began my final descent prior to landing. I kept the flarepath in view until I suddenly realised that I could not longer see it ahead. Simultaneously, a red Very flare exploded in the air. I opened the throttle and climbed a little higher –whereupon I saw the flarepath once again. I crossed the threshold and plonked her down on her main undercarriage leaving the tailwheel to drop when it felt like it'.

As he climbed out of the cockpit covered in sweat the night flying officer said, 'Do you know that you were in five feet of the ground when I shot off the flare and if there had been a tree in your path, it would have been curtains for you?'

Sgt James Pickering made his first night flight in a Spitfire more by accident than design. Having carried out a number of patrols from Hawkinge, the dozen Spitfires of 64 Sqn were ordered back to their main base at Kenley.

'It was dusk when we eventually took off one after another. The Brighton to London railway line was our only navigation aid as accurate map reading was impossible, even with the cockpit lights turned down to the minimum. The blackout was almost total throughout Southeast England at the time. The only way that we could find Kenley was by catching sight of a chance light that

flashed in Morse code the position of our particular airfield. Having found this, it was somewhat daunting to discover that due to the wind direction, the shortest runway at Kenley was being used for the night landing. The only landing aid, apart from the flarepath, was the officer in charge of night flying's Aldis lamp which flashed green when you were OK to land, and red when you were too high, or low, on your approach. It was amazing that all the pilots got down that night in one piece.'

One Battle of Britain ace proved that it was not only possible to fly the Spitfire at night, but also to fight with it. South African former merchant seaman, Adolph Gysbert 'Sailor' Malan gained a RAF commission in 1936. In May 1940, he shot down two enemy aircraft in his first mission over Dunkirk while flying a Spitfire with 74 (Tiger) Sqn.

Above: The newly posted P/O Leon Collingridge poses with his 66 Sqn Spitfire Ia at Duxford. Spitfire N3042 was destroyed during the Battle of Britain but the pilot survived.

Below: Groundcrews have already started the engines as pilots of 611 Sqn scramble at an alert during the 'Phoney War' period in the winter of 1939/40.

GROUNDCREW AND WEAPONS

'ERKS'

The introduction of the Spitfire represented a leap in technology for the RAF groundcrews as well as the pilots. In a short space of time, and with little specialist training, they had to come to terms with V12 Merlins, stressed skin, split flaps, hydraulics, pneumatics and electrics. Like their aircrew colleagues who were called to duty on 24 August 1939, the Aircraftsmen Mechanics came from diverse backgrounds ranging from ex-Royal Flying Corps reservists, RAF apprentices ('brats') and direct entry regulars. They had a few months to adjust to the new high technology fighters that were about to defend Great Britain against almost certain invasion.

Right: A 19 squadron Spitfire Ia with the engine covers off giving easy access to the 'erks' when working on its Rolls-Royce Merlin engine and its oil and coolant tanks.

RAF ground crews, or 'erks' as they were known, had already been bloodied in the Battle of France where many lost their lives or were captured. Now they were again in the front line as the Battle of Britain gathered momentum. Often moved at a few hours notice, the ground crews had to take whatever accommodation they could –in many cases tents or the outhouses of the local stately home vacated for the duration by its owners. At the height of the battle, squadrons were flying up to four or five sorties a day. When the Spitfires landed they were expected to be refuelled, re-armed

Below: Groundcrews refuel and re-arm 12 Group's chocked Spitfires of 66 Sqn after a patrol during the initial phase of the Battle of Britain.

with gun ports taped, have their engines checked, oil and glycol coolant tanks topped up, oxygen cylinders replaced and radio tested, all within ten minutes!

Early Spitfires had to have their eight Browning machine guns washed in a petrol solution to prevent them jamming at high altitudes, while at the same time lubricated in oil to stop them rusting. Repairs and routine maintenance had to be carried out in the open during bad weather, when flying was cancelled, or at night in the blackout. During night raids in the area, power and water mains were often knocked out of

Left: A groundcrew fills the Spitfire's top tank with 48 gallons of 100 octane fuel while another checks the socket for the external battery starter lead.

Right: An 'erk' paints the name of 65 Sqn on to the nose of a Spitfire II. Others had names of companies and individuals who had presented a Spitfire to the nation.

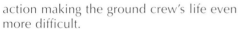

Right: One of the 'erks' less popular tasks was holding down the tail while the Spitfire's engine is opened up to full revs.

Below: Groundcrews 'walking out' Spitfires of 609 Sqn to make sure they are clear of each other aircraft before they taxi for take-off.

action making the ground crew's life even more difficult.

In August and September 11 Group's main fighter bases came under attack by the *Luftwaffe* and ground crew helped man the airfield defence anti-aircraft guns. These raids often destroyed accommodation blocks and killed many aircraftsmen, and women. When the raids were over, airfield damage was repaired by the groundcrews before they moved to the base's satellite field where their squadron's Spitfires were operating.

When at a state of readiness, a member of the groundcrew, the engine fitter, would warm up the Spitfire's engine at regular

intervals while the other member of the 'team', the airframe rigger, would be ready to help the pilot into his parachute and strap him into the seat in the event of a scramble.

The Merlin engines fitted to the first RAF Spitfires had to be started by using an external battery power mounted on a trolley accumulator manhandled into place by the groundcrew. The Spitfire II's engine was fitted with an internal Koffman cartridge starter.

Most pilots appreciated his groundcrew's part in his ability to operate effectively. A smooth running engine, clean and well oiled canopy and non-jamming guns would often not only increase his chances of shooting down the enemy, but could be the difference between life and death.

WEAPONS

Designed as an agile air defence fighter, the Spitfires that took part in the Battle of Britain had no provision for carrying any armament other than internal guns.

The original Spitfire, the unsuccessful F7/30 was armed with four .303 machine guns but thanks to a S/L R S Storey of the Air Ministry's Operational Requirements Branch, the number of guns was doubled in AM Specification F37/34 which led directly to the Battle of Britain Spitfire. S/L Storey had proved in trials that a target aircraft could be destroyed in a few seconds when fired on by eight guns putting out not less than 1,000 rounds per minute.

To achieve this requirement, the Air

Below: A team of armourers open the Spitfire's numerous access doors to replace the Browning's ammunition boxes during re-arming.

Ministry negotiated the rights to build a modified version of the US Colt-Browning .30 machine gun in 1935. The main difference from the US design was that the British gun, 2,000 of which were built every week by the Birmingham Small Arms company (BSA) in 1940, had to be modified to use the British standard rimmed .303 (7.7 mm) calibre round with corresponding alterations to the ammunition feed system. After initial snags, the gun proved to a first class weapon.

The 44.5 inch (1130 mm) long gun weighed 22 lbs (10 kg), had a muzzle velocity of 2,660 feet per second (811 m/s), and carried 300 rounds which fired at a rate of 1,200 per minute. This meant that the Spitfire pilot using his eight guns could fire

160 rounds in a one second burst. A full burst of eight guns could scrub almost 25 mph off the flying speed and lower the nose, as though the landing flaps had been extended.

RAF regulations at the outbreak of war stated that the eight guns should be set up to converge at 650 yards (594 m) although many experienced pilots such as 'Al' Deere and 'Sailor' Malan calibrated their guns to converge at only 250 yards (229 m).

Before radiator heat was ducted into the gun bays, the Brownings were prone to jamming in icing conditions although taping over the gun ports prevented this until after the guns were fired.

The ammunition used was a mix of armour-piercing, tracer and incendiary. Following a last minute deal in 1939, the Air Ministry purchased the rights to manufacture the Belgian designed De Wilde combined armour-piercing and incendiary bullet for £30,000. The Brownings installed in the Spitfire I and II were widely spaced and staggered to enabled them to be fitted in the thin elliptical 'A' wing. When re-arming the Spitfire the armourers had to open a total of 22 gun bay and ammunition panels held by 150 turnbuttons. (The Hawker Hurricane had only two panels and 32 turnbuttons). Nevertheless, a team of four experienced armourers could re-arm the Spitfire and re-tape the gunports in less than 15 minutes.

Although many Browning guns were converted from the Mark II to Mark II Star with a slightly increased rate of fire, many considered that the Spitfire was outgunned by the Bf 109E which was armed with two MG 17 7.9 mm machine guns each carrying 1,000 rounds, plus two MG FF 20 mm cannon each with 60 rounds. In response to this perceived disadvantage, the Spitfire's wing was redesigned to accommodate a 20 mm cannon with sixty shells in a drum-type magazine in place of two of the Brownings. Known as the 'B' wing, it was fitted to 30 Mk I aircraft on the production line which were issued to 19 Sqn in August 1940. The gun selected was the Hispano-Suiza 20 mm Oerlikon cannon, ironically the same gun as used by the *Luftwaffe* Bf 109Es. A licence agreement was purchased and the first of 45,582 Hispano cannons built during World War II was delivered from the BSA factory at Sparkbrook in April 1940.

Shoehorning the 52.8 in (1341 mm) long cannon into the thin wing proved a problem and a blister fairing had to be fitted over the ammunition feed drums. The Hispano Mk I cannon was also plagued by frequent

SPITFIRE ARMAMENT

Early Spitfires carried eight .303 Browning machine guns, but experience showed that heavier weapons were required. The only drawback to the 20 mm cannon was that ammunition supply was rather limited, so a continuation of cannon and machine guns was tried on some marks.

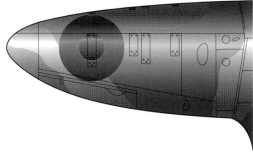

Right: Battle of Britain Spitfire I and IIa were fitted with the A-Wing with 4 x .303 Colt Browning machine guns.

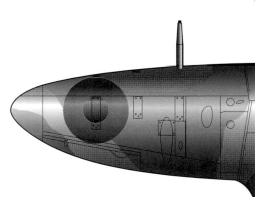

Right: The B-Wing with 1 x 20 mm Hispano cannon and 2 x .303 Colt Browning machine guns was fitted to Spitfire IIbs and early Vs.

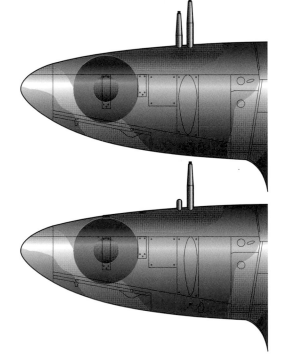

Right: The first Spitfire fitted with the 2 x 20 mm Hispano cannon C-Wing was the F.21 which first flew in 1944.

Right: The Universal Wing was fitted to Seafire I/II variants with a 20 mm Hispano cannon and 2 x .303 Browning machine guns.

Above: Spitfire Ia N3072 of 611 Sqn spits out spent .303 casings and belt links as the pilot harmonises his eight Brownings in the butts at Digby.

Right: A fitter wearing his 'tin hat' helps a 66 Sqn pilot strap into the cockpit. Note the armoured windscreen, flush rear view mirror and S/L markings below the cockpit.

jamming caused by an unreliable feed mechanism and ejectors. The Spitfire Ibs were unpopular with their pilots who considered a total firing period of only six seconds, if the gun did not jam, too short for accurate aiming. Although a prototype cannon-armed Spitfire shot down a Dornier Do 17 in March 1940, the new gun's teething problems were not ironed out until after the Battle of Britain was over.

A few operational Spitfires were fitted with a cine camera gun in the starboard wing root in time for the Battle of Britain. These were designed to be used to verify kills but even when fitted were prone to malfunctioning at the vital moments.

Protection for the pilot was fairly basic in the early Spitfires, restricted to only a two inch (51 mm) thick glass windscreen and a quarter-inch (6.35 mm) stainless steel plate behind the pilot's seat. Following battle damage suffered during the Dunkirk evacuation, armoured glycol coolant tanks and self sealing lower fuel tanks –located in front for the pilot's legs –were fitted in the field during the Battle of Britain. Fireproof bulkheads behind the pilot and jettisonable canopies were not fitted until after the Battle was over.

Above: 'Erks' defend their ears as a 72 Sqn Spitfire Ia harmonises its eight Brownings at Acklington in 1940.

Below: Armourers servicing a 20 mm Hispano cannon mounted in the B-Wing which was fitted to some Spitfire I/IIbs in the Battle.

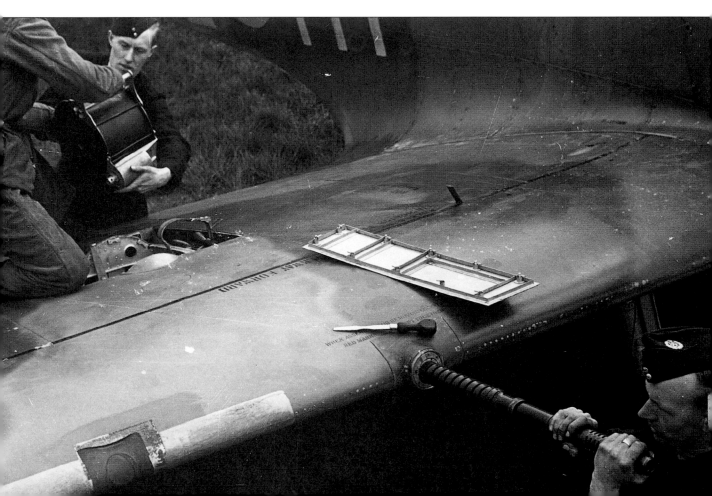

INTO BATTLE
GROUND CONTROL

The first phase of the Battle of Britain began on 10 July 1940. Under Air Chief Marshal Dowding, Fighter Command was divided into groups, the most important of which would be No 11 Group which covered the south-east of England –the front line; No 12 Group defended central England, No 10 Group the south-west, No 13 Group from Yorkshire to Scotland.

Dowding was an austere and remote figure to his young fighter pilots, who nicknamed him 'Stuffy'. The 11 Group commander, Air Vice Marshal Keith Park was popular and approachable. A tough New Zealander, Park

was a First World War RFC fighter pilot who had shot down 20 enemy aircraft. Promoted over the head of 12 Group's commander Air Vice Marshal Trafford Leigh-Mallory, an ambitious career officer who would come into conflict Dowding as the Battle progressed, Park made regular and informal visits to front line units flying his own Hurricane.

Each Group was further divided into sectors surrounding the main fighter bases which were known as Sector Stations. To cope with extra squadrons being moved towards the Battle front, or when under attack, many of these Sector Stations had one of more 'satellite' airfields. All Fighter Command airfields were protected by anti-aircraft guns manned by the Army and RAF Aircraftsmen. Dowding also had the foresight to establish a

Right: A 350ft Chain Home Low (CHL) mast with rotating aerial mounted on the top used to search for low-flying enemy aircraft, a vital part of Britain's air defence in 1940.

Left: A WAAF radar observer watching 'blips' on a cathode ray tube in the receiver hut of a Chain Home radar station, details of which were phoned to Fighter Command's Control Room.

Below: An Observer Corps post in 1940 with the observer using a device to measure the altitude and heading of enemy aircraft.

network for operations rooms which collated information from radar stations and observers sent down dedicated telephone lines.

After the Radio Direction Finding (RDF) experiments in the 1935, the decision was taken to build a chain of radar stations covering the south and east coasts of Britain, the first of which was opened at Dover in 1937. At the start of the Battle there were 21 Chain Home (CH) stations in operation. They could detect aircraft at heights between 5 and 20,000 feet (1524-6096 m) at up to 120 miles (192 km). In addition, 30 Chain Home Low (CHL) stations could detect aircraft flying below 5,000 feet at a maximum range of 50 miles (80 km). The radar aerials were mounted on towers 350 feet (107 m) high: those on the south coast could be seen from France. Vital to the defence of Britain they became priority targets for the *Luftwaffe*. Mobile Radar Units (MLU) with a maximum range of 90 miles (144 km) were bought into operation during

the Battle to supplement fixed sites or those put temporarily out of action by air attacks.

The Observer Corps, made up of volunteer 'skywatchers', was established in September 1938 as a direct result of the Munich Crisis. Many of these volunteers were ex-service men and women, although by the outbreak of war it was commanded by full-time officers. On the eve of the Battle of Britain some 30,000 observers manned more than 1,000 posts reporting to 32 centres. Aircraft recognition was all important. While radar stations gave accurate information about the range of enemy aircraft, pinpointing their altitude was more difficult and verification often fell to the observers using simple but effective measuring devices. They were also used to track enemy formations that had passed over the radar stations –which only looked one way. On cloudy days, the observers had to rely on sound alone to identify aircraft's altitude and bearing.

All these reports were fed to the 'filter' room at Fighter Command's headquarters at Bentley Priory located in the suburbs of north London. There, all unidentified aircraft reports, known as 'X-raids', were plotted, numbered and displayed on coloured markers which were moved across a large map table by WAAF plotters using long rakes. As soon as an enemy formation's size, bearing and altitude was confirmed, the information was passed to Sector Operations Rooms by landline.

Here these 'X-raid' plots were tracked on a map table showing the sector, its fighter airfields and squadrons at Readiness and 15 minutes Available at each one and their status. As soon as the plot was identified as an enemy formation, the Sector Controller, himself a experienced former or resting fighter pilot, would scramble one or more squadrons to intercept the raiders.

Spitfire squadrons were divided into two flights of six aircraft which in turn were split into sections of three. Each squadron had a codename, each flight a letter 'A' or 'B', each section a colour and each section pilot a number. The Controller would 'scramble 'Diamond Squadron', 'Red' and 'Green' sections 'B' flight. He would communicate with the flight commander –'Diamond leader' by radio telephone, or R/T, a high frequency (HF) radio which had a limited range and was subject to interference and distortion. However, very high frequency (VHF) radio with a range of 100 miles (160 km) would not be fully developed and in quantity production until after the Battle was over. When scrambled, the flight commander would be given an altitude to climb to ('angels') and a heading to steer ('vector') to intercept the unidentified aircraft ('bogeys') by the Sector Controller as he watched the plotters moving markers across the map table. The flight commander would be in direct communication with his pilots identified as 'Red One' or 'Blue Two'. When the formation was sighted and identified as hostile ('bandits') he would call 'Tally-Ho' and the fight would begin.

Above: Three sections of 610 Sqn flying a readiness patrol in July 1940. Spitfire Ia DW-K was damaged beyond repair by a Bf 109 near Dover in August.

LET BATTLE COMMENCE

For the first weeks of the Battle, three *Luftwaffe* Air Fleets, *Luftflotte* 2 in north-western France and the Low Countries, *Luftflotte* 3 in east and central France and *Luftflotte* 5 based in Norway and Denmark, concentrated on attacking British shipping. During this phase, only five Spitfire squadrons were assigned to 11 Group, three of which were based at RAF Hornchurch.

Spitfires enjoyed considerable success against Junkers Ju 87 Stuka dive bombers, which attacked coastal convoys in the Channel, and their Bf 110 escorts. But the opening of the battle was not without loss. No 54 Squadron flew a total of 504 sorties in July, and lost five pilots plus another three wounded, with 12 Spitfires destroyed. By 8 August, when the *Luftwaffe* switched its attacks to coastal airfields and radar stations, more than 60 Spitfires had been lost, but the first Mk IIas from Castle Bromwich were being delivered to front line units. There were also eight Spitfire squadrons now in 11 Group.

As a build up to *Alder Tag* (Eagle Day) –the destruction of Fighter Command scheduled for 13 August –the *Luftwaffe* flew more than 1,000 sorties a day carrying out a series of low level attacks on convoys in the Thames Estuary and off East Anglia, radar stations at

Dover (dubbed 'Hellfire Corner'), Ventnor on the Isle of Wight and Hawkinge, Lympne and Manston airfields. In response, squadrons from 10, 11 and 12 Groups were thrown into the action.

Weather on *Alder Tag* led to a number of *Luftwaffe* attacks to be cancelled although by the end of the day it had mounted 1,485 sorties against Fighter Command's 700. One of the highlights of the day for the defenders, was the shooting down of six out of nine Stukas attacking the Ventnor radar station by Spitfires of 609 Sqn based at Middle Wallop.

However, two days later, the *Luftwaffe* could have succeeded in inflicting a mortal blow on Fighter Command when it committed all three Air Fleets to the Battle. He 111s and Ju 88s of *Luftflotte* 5 attacked airfields in 12 and 13 Groups while *Luftflotten* 2 and 3 mounted large raids on targets in 10 and 11 Groups. In more that 1,700 sorties, the *Luftwaffe* caused considerable damage to airfields, radar stations and the Short Brothers aircraft factory in the south, but their bombers suffered badly from 13 Group's fighters over the North Sea. The day's action resulted in the transfer of *Luftflotte* 5's remaining bomber strength to the

Below: A Blenheim IF of 29 Sqn at Digby in 12 Group. The type was outclassed by the Bf 109 and withdrawn from day operations at the end of August.

Air Fleets in France, and the complete withdrawal of Stuka units, which had suffered unacceptable losses.

Heavy raids on airfields continued for another week with Hurricane and Spitfire squadrons having to fly up to five patrols a day during the long daylight hours of August. As a general rule, the Hurricanes were tasked with intercepting the bomber formations which typically flew between 12-20,000 feet (3658-6096 m) while the Spitfires attacked the protective layers of Bf 109s flying 5-10,000 feet (1524-3048 m) above the bombers.

When bad weather provided a lull in the battle, the cost of the previous ten weeks fierce fighting became clear. Almost 100 Fighter Command pilots had been killed or were missing; another 60 were wounded and temporarily out of action. In response to the

death of many pilots who baled out over the sea, an RAF co-ordinated air-sea rescue organisation was established using RAF launches, Lysander Army Co-operation aircraft and a few Walrus amphibians. As a short term measure to combat the shortage of pilots, Lysander and Battle light bomber pilots were transferred to Fighter Command, sent on a six day course at the Harwarden OTU and posted to front line fighter squadrons. In the same period more than 50 Spitfires had been destroyed and another 40 badly damaged in the air and on the ground. Six airfields, including Kenley, Croydon and Biggin Hill, were badly damaged and hundreds of airmen and women killed or wounded by the air raids.

The *Luftwaffe* had lost over 200 aircraft, mostly bombers, and decided to change its

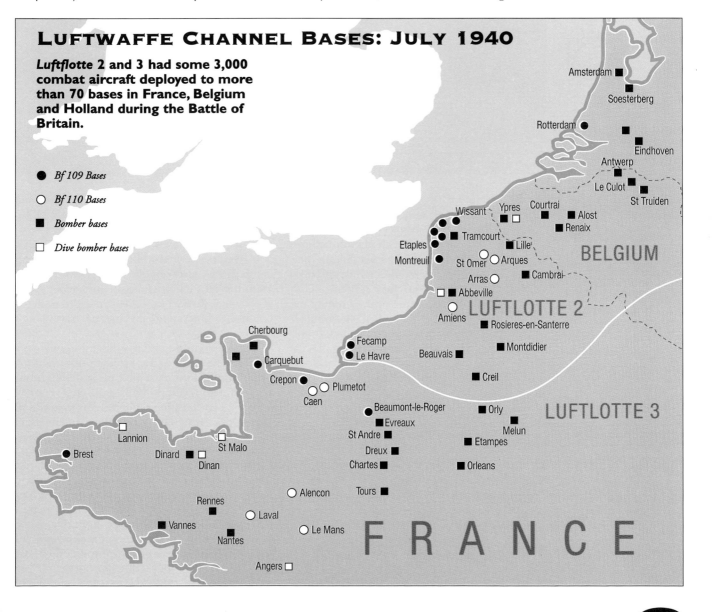

LUFTWAFFE CHANNEL BASES: JULY 1940

Luftflotte **2 and 3 had some 3,000 combat aircraft deployed to more than 70 bases in France, Belgium and Holland during the Battle of Britain.**

● *Bf 109 Bases*

○ *Bf 110 Bases*

■ *Bomber bases*

□ *Dive bomber bases*

Above: This KG.76 Do 17E-2 was shot down near Biggin Hill afer a low-level raid on Kenley airfield on 18 August. The crew escaped with injuries.

tactics in all out effort to bring the RAF to its knees. Its attacks would now concentrate of 11 Group airfields that formed a protective ring around London. Also, the escorting Bf 109s would fly much closer to the bomber formations to enable them to fight off the RAF interceptors before they had a chance to shoot down the raiders. Both of these measures were to produce immediate and positive results for the *Luftwaffe*. On 24 August Manston was almost put out of action when over 100 bombers attacked. At the same time Hornchurch and North Weald air-fields were accurately targeted by *Luftflotte* 2.

This pattern of heavy raids by large formations of well protected bombers continued throughout August. On 30 August, Fighter Command flew over 1,000 sorties for the first time, but the following day it suffered its worst losses to date. The *Luftwaffe* mounted a total of 1,300 sorties that left Hornchurch and Biggin Hill extensively damaged while in the battles in the skies overhead, 39 RAF fighters were shot down

and 14 pilots killed with another 10 Spitfires destroyed on the ground. German losses were 41 aircraft. Squadrons in 11 Group were now at full stretch while the opportunities for them to rotate with those in other groups to rest and replace lost pilots and aircraft, were becoming fewer by the week.

At the beginning of September, Dowding was forced to re-classify Fighter Command squadrons. All those in 11 Group, Duxford in 10 Group and Middle Wallop in 10 Group were now 'A' squadrons, and the remainder in 10 and 12 Groups became 'B' squadrons. All other units were designated as 'C' squadrons to be used as advanced OTUs preparing newly qualified pilots for posting to 'A' squadrons.

In the two weeks from 24 August, 466 RAF fighters were destroyed or damaged, nearly 200 more than were delivered from the factories or CROs. Potentially more serious was the fact that 103 pilots were killed or missing and with only 190 new pilots available to replace them.

Typical of the 11 Group's Spitfire squadrons were 603 Sqn which lost 16 aircraft and 12 pilots, and 616 Sqn which lost 12 aircraft and five pilots and had to be withdrawn from the Battle. On 30 August alone, 222 Sqn at Hornchurch lost no less than eight of its Spitfires.

As many as 750 German bombers attacked British airfields on every day of the first week in September and although more than 100 of them were shot down during this phase of the Battle, they managed to inflict heavy damage to six of the seven sector stations and five satellite airfields. Fighter Command was now struggling to keep the *Luftwaffe* at bay. Unexpectedly, *Reichmarschall* Herman Göring, First World War fighter ace and *Luftwaffe* Commander-in-Chief, was about to come to its rescue.

Despite its apparent success in recent weeks, the *Luftwaffe* had failed to annihilate the RAF's fighter force and the scheduled date of Operation *Seelöwe* –the invasion of Britain, was looking less creditable as the weeks of fighting wore on. It was postponed until 17 September.

Göring blamed his fighter units for failing to gain air superiority over Fighter Command. In reality, the fact that the capable Bf 109s were tied to the slow and unwieldy bomber formations and were at the limit of their range when they met the defending fighters, seriously reduced their effectiveness. Nevertheless, Göring decided to commit all

the Air Fleets in France and Low Countries to a massive attack on one key target –London.

On 7 September more than 300 bombers escorted by 600 fighters bombed the East End of London. Combat in the air was as fierce as ever with both sides suffering heavy losses, but significantly Fighter Command's airfields were intact and its groundcrews could service the fighters without air raid sirens interrupting their vital work.

London was not the only British city to be attacked in September 1940. Southampton, Portsmouth, Bristol and Plymouth were all targeted by German bombers. But it was a series of heavy raids on London on 15 September that would prove to be a decisive turning point in the Battle. The weather was clear and sunny. The German formations flew higher than usual but on the day more than 300 RAF fighters were thrown into action. Although there were problems co-ordinating the large numbers of aircraft from two different Groups, 11 and 12, some 60 German aircraft were shot down for the loss of 26 RAF fighters. Seven of these were Spitfires but eight new or repaired aircraft were delivered to squadrons the same day. Two days later Operation *Seelöwe* was postponed indefinitely.

Weather was now becoming a factor in the Battle. Massed raids were replaced by 'hit and run' attacks by smaller formations of Me 110 and Bf 109 fighter-bombers. At the end of September the Ju 88s and He 111s returned

Below: A section of 92 Sqn Spitfires line-up for take-off from Biggin Hill in September for a patrol over the south coast.

Above: The Spitfire's exceptionally strong elliptical wing was capable of surviving extensive damage from the Bf 109's cannon fire.

in force to attack aircraft factories in southern England. On 25 September the Bristol Aeroplane works at Filton was put out of action for some weeks by a raid that killed or injured more than 250 people. The following day, the *Luftwaffe* turned its attention to Supermarine's Woolston factory. A precision raid by 75 bombers devastated the factory and killed 30 on its staff in the process. As the Germans turned for home, they were attacked by Spitfires from three squadrons, 152 and 609 in 10 Group, and 602 in 11 Group. In

the ensuing fight, only three of the raiders were shot down for the loss of six RAF fighters including two Spitfires.

Although only three completed Spitfires were destroyed in the raid, a number of others on the production lines were badly damaged and production was bought to a halt for more than a week. Total Spitfire production dropped from 133 in August to 59 in October.

The Battle of Britain officially continued until 31 October when the *Luftwaffe* resorted

to night attacks– 'the Blitz'. The RAF had won a close run, and costly victory. During October 325 German aircraft were shot down but Fighter Command lost 100 pilots with another 85 wounded.

Nearly 3,000 Allied pilots from 14 different nations took part in the Battle of Britain. More than 500 were killed and another 500 wounded. A total of 326 Spitfires were destroyed in the four month Battle with another 589 damaged –808 new aircraft were delivered from the factories. However Spitfire squadrons were credited with 521 confirmed victories.

Although the Hurricane bore the brunt of the fighting – there were more of them available – the Spitfire was undoubtedly the 'star of the show' in the public's mind. In any event, it all came down to the outstanding flying and leadership qualities of Fighter Command's pilots.

Within a month of the end of the Battle, the team that engineered Fighter Command's victory was broken up. Air Vice Marshal Keith Park was relieved of the command of 11 Group and posted to Flying Training Command. His long-time rival Leigh-Mallory took over 11 Group. Park's boss Air Chief Marshall Sir Hugh Dowding was summarily retired both from his post and the RAF. At the end of the year Lord Beaverbrook, who had been accused of causing disruption to established procedures, was moved to the Ministry of Supply.

Above: Many Spitfire IIs produced during July and September 1940 were 'presentation' aircraft, paid for by countries, companies or the general public.

Left: This Bf 109E-3 of JG.3 crash landed in a field in Kent on 5 September has 13 'kill' marks on the tail and belonged to Lt von Werra, the only Luftwaffe pilot to escape to Germany.

BROTHERS IN ARMS

Left: The Hawker Hurricane was the senior partner in Fighter Command's air defence of Britain having won its battle spurs in Norway and France.

Below: A Hurricane in the markings of 257 Sqn which flew from Northolt close to Fighter Command Headquarters in the early phases of the Battle of Britain.

Hawker Hurricane

Whereas the Spitfire had more charisma, the tough Hurricane was the workhorse of the Battle of Britain. In July 1940, the 32 Fighter Command squadrons were flying the Hurricane Mk 1 against *Luftwaffe* bombers. Like the Spitfire, it began as a private venture, designed by Sydney Camm, Hawker's chief designer. The Hurricane I entered RAF service with 111 Sqn in 1937 was powered by the same 1,030hp Merlin III as the Spitfire Ia and had the same armament –eight .303 Browning machine guns. It was heavier, slower and less agile than its more famous partner but the Hurricane's rugged construction, forgiving flying qualities and tremendous ability to absorb battle damage, made it popular with its pilots. It was an extremely stable gun platform and its fabric covered fuselage was easy to repair.

Fighter Command Hurricanes shot down a total of 655 enemy aircraft during the Battle of Britain. The RAF's first line strength of Hurricane Mk 1s during the battle averaged 530 with some 200 new aircraft leaving the factories every month between July and October. After its success in the Battle of Britain, the Hurricane went on the fight with distinction in Russia and the Mediterranean and Far East. The last of more than 14,000 Hurricanes was delivered to the RAF in September 1944.

Above: A Boulton Paul Defiant Mk 1 flown by the CO of 264 Sqn which flew with 12 Group before being withdrawn from day operations at the end of August.

Right: The Defiant opened its score as a night fighter on 16 September when 141 Sqn aircraft shot down two He 111s and a KG.54 Ju 88 on the following night.

Boulton Paul Defiant

The only other single-engine monoplane fighter to serve with Fighter Command during the Battle of Britain was the Defiant Mk 1. Originally developed as an anti-bomber fighter, the Defiant, which first flew in August 1937 was similar in size to the Hurricane, powered by the same Merlin III engine but differed radically in its armament.
Its firepower came from a manned power-operated turret fitted behind the pilot's cockpit. It had no forward firing guns. The four .303 Browning machine gun turret was used with great success when the Defiants of 264 Sqn first went into action over Dunkirk in May 1940. In only a few days the squadron claimed 65 kills, 38 of them on one day!

However, by the opening phase of the Battle of Britain, *Luftwaffe* fighter pilots had learned to attack the Defiants head-on. The vulnerable two-seaters, which had a lower top speed that the Hurricane, soon suffered heavy losses. On 19 July, 141 Sqn lost six of its nine Defiants to Bf 109s. The type was soon withdrawn from daylight operations although the Defiant went on to have a second career as a night fighter. More than 1,000 Defiants were produced and they finished their service life with Air-Sea Rescue units.

Above: Blenheim IF K7159 was a veteran of the Battle of Britain before adopting the black overall finish of a night fighter OTU.

Below: Like the Defiant, the Blenheim IF suffered badly at the hands of Bf 109s and was withdrawn from day operations. This 604 Sqn aircraft based at Middle Wallop is fitted with a ventral gun pack.

Bristol Blenheim

The Bristol Blenheim was yet another example of the RAF being 'sponsored' by wealthy patriot. In this case it was the newspaper magnate Lord Rothermere who agreed to underwrite the cost of a high performance all metal eight-seat airliner designed by the Bristol Aeroplane Company. The performance of the twin-engined Bristol 142, christened 'Britain First' which first flew in 1935 was so impressive that the RAF asked to test it and Lord Rothermere presented it to the nation.

The Type 142 was originally developed into the Blenheim light bomber, the first of which flew on 25 July 1936. As war loomed, the Air Ministry ordered some 200 aircraft to be converted to long-range day fighters by fitting four .303 Browning machine guns in a ventral gun pack. As with the Defiant, the Blenheim IF proved to be no match for the Bf 109. With a crew of two, and powered by two 840hp Bristol Mercury VIII radial engines the Blenheim IF's top speed was only 260 mph.

Seven Fighter Command squadrons, with some 50 Blenheim IFs between them, remained in the front line of the Battle with 11 Group until the end of August. But their limited performance led to their withdrawal from day operations. As with the Defiant, they made useful night fighters, especially when fitted with the first airborne radar sets.

Gloster Gladiator

The last of the RAF's biplane fighters, the Gladiator was obsolete at the outbreak of the War. However, it was to be involved in some epic battles against the Axis powers long after its should have been withdrawn from service. Powered by 840 hp Mercury IX radial engine which gave it a maximum speed of 253mph, the single-seat Gladiator was armed with four .303 Browning machine guns, two in the nose and two under the wings. Having first entered RAF service with 72 Sqn on 22 February 1937, Fighter Command had four first-line Gladiator squadrons at the outbreak of hostilities. Fighter Command's first aerial victory came on 17 October 1939 when Gladiator Is of 607 (County of Durham) Squadron shot down a Do 18 flying boat off the Yorkshire coast.

Only one Gladiator unit fought in the Battle of Britain. Gladiator IIs of 247 Sqn assigned to 10 Group for local defences of the Royal Naval Dockyards at Plymouth. Although scrambled on a numerous of occasions, no enemy aircraft were claimed, but no Gladiators were lost in combat. A flight of Sea

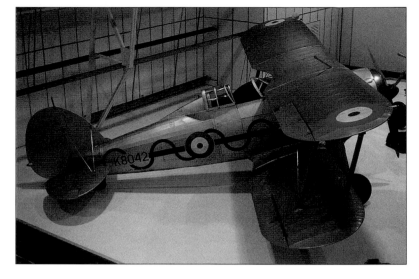

Gladiators from 804 Sqn Fleet Air Arm saw action with 13 Group in July 1940 flying alongside Fighter Command Hurricanes at Wick. Overseas, RAF pilots continued to fly the ageing but agile biplane fighter into combat until it was finally withdrawn from front line units at the end of 1941.

Above: Four first line Fighter Command squadrons were equipped with the Gloster Gladiator in September 1939 but 87 Sqn, whose pre-war colours adorn this aircraft, had re-equipped with Hurricanes.

Left: A Gladiator II of 247 Sqn based at Roborough in 10 Group throughout the Battle of Britain tasked with the air defence of Royal Naval dockyards at Plymouth.

THE SORTIE

Described variously by those who flew it as 'a thoroughbred', 'like riding a responsive mount', 'a real lady' and 'too beautiful to be a fighting machine', the Spitfire was nevertheless designed and built as a weapon of war. As such, a few hundred of these advanced fighters were dispersed at a dozen Sector Stations and their satellite airfields during the summer months of 1940 waiting for the signal to go into battle against German fighters and bombers.

Scramble! The call from an ops clerk holding a telephone was the signal for the pilots to drop books, playing cards and mugs of tea and knock chairs over as they grab flying kit and race for their Spitfires fanned out around the dispersal hut.

For these young pilots at dawn readiness, the day began four hours earlier with a batman shaking them awake after only a few hours sleep following their last sortie of the previous evening. After a quick cup of tea and a wash they hurry to the waiting motor transport that takes them to the blacked-out crew-room/dispersal hut. Here amongst the clutter of magazines, pilots' notes, maps, unwashed mugs and full ashtrays, an airman attempts to light a iron stove. Although it is the summer, there is a distinct chill in the air at dawn. The pilots check the 'Readiness' board for their allotted aircraft and the order of flying.

On another notice board is the met forecast pinned up amongst routine station orders and notices: clear and warm with high scattered clouds. They can be scrambled at anytime after first light.

The 'Readiness' pilots wait for the call dressed in a variety of unofficial kit. At this time of year all wear crumpled uniforms, some over shirts and ties, others over a roll-neck pullover while a few have girl-friend's silk scarves around their necks. Most wear standard issue shiny, or not so shiny, black shoes while some prefer leather flying boots, usually with crumpled maps tucked in the tops. In winter they would be wearing an Irvin flying suit or sheepskin flying jacket over their uniform. All wear a yellow-dyed canvas 'Mae West' life jacket (named after an ample-bosomed Hollywood film star of the period) which has to be blown up by mouth in the event of an emergency.

The most important survival equipment for a Spitfire pilot is his parachute. This is usually taken out and fitted into the bucket seat well before take-off. Other items of flying clothing such as leather gloves, which few pilots wear, the soft leather helmet with built-in earphones, goggles and chamois lined combined oxygen mask and microphone are often left draped over the trailing edge of the wing.

The squadron's nine serviceable Spitfires at readiness are positioned around the 'readiness' hut in order of seniority. The flight commander's aircraft is the nearest and the 'sprog's' (new pilot) is furthest away. One of the squadron is a former winner of the Le Mans 24 Hour race where the drivers have to sprint across the track to their car from the pits when the starting flag drops. He is usually the first to be airborne when scrambled.

A hundred miles away, *Luftwaffe* bomber crews are preparing to launch the first attacks of the day from their airfields in Normandy. There is little talk between the pilots. Some have curled up on the broken settee and fallen asleep. A shrill telephone bell shattered the silence. After a few mumbled words, the 'erk' replaces the 'blower'

'Nothing yet, sir.'

The pilots grown and resume their interrupted card game or cat-nap.

At 8.00 hours the telephone rings again.

'Scramble nine aircraft. Patrol Rye. Angels three zero.'

Red, Yellow and Blue section pilots sprint out of the hut while the remainder stand around the door and watch the action. As Diamond Blue leader races towards his camouflaged Spitfire Ia, 'D-Delta', his fitter is already in the cockpit firing up the Rolls Royce Merlin while his rigger hands him his helmet, goggles and gloves. Blue leader jumps on the port wing as the fitter slides out of the cockpit to help strap him in. First the parachute straps, then the lap, shoulder and legs straps of the Sutton Harness are clipped into the Quick Release box.

Far left: The Controller on the R/T in the Sector Operations Room at Duxford in 12 Group. Note the 'Careless talk costs lives' poster pinned to front of his dais.

Above right: An 'erk' takes a message on the 'blower' in the squadron's crew-room cum dispersal hut with the 'readiness' board to his left.

Right: Following a 'scramble' call, a pilot races to his Spitfire where his fitter is already in the cockpit starting the Merlin while the rigger stands on the wing ready to strap him in.

THE COCKPIT

Smaller than that of the Gladiator or Hurricane, the Spitfire's cockpit is compact, but comfortable for all but the largest pilot. The 'bubble' canopy, the first of its type, plus the additional perspex area behind the pilot's headrest affords excellent all round visibility compared with other fighters. Another invaluable aid for the fighter pilot is the rear-view mirror fitted to all Spitfires at the beginning of the Battle of Britain. The seat can be raised for take-off and landing although forward visibility on the ground is still restricted by the long nose.

In an emergency the Spitfire can be abandoned with the canopy slid fully back and the port side door flap down. However the canopy is difficult to open at speeds over 250 mph and the pilot may have to resort to using the crowbar clipped inside the door flap to smash it open. Canopy jettison gear has not yet been fitted to Battle of Britain Spitfires.

The cockpit instrument panel is dominated by state-of-the-art controls and switches. Apart from the standard flight instruments –artificial horizon, direction indicator, turn and bank indicator, rate of climb and descent indicator and altimeter –and fuel and engine temperature and pressure gauges which are recognisable in all other types of aircraft since 1918, many are not. These include the reflector sight switch, R/T and oxygen sockets, camera gun master switch, airscrew pitch control and flap and undercarriage control levers. The latter is located on the right-hand side of the cockpit which means that the pilot has to move his left hand from the throttle to the control column to operate the hydraulic undercarriage control lever with his right hand. In early Spitfire Mark 1s this was a two foot-long handle which had to be pumped vigorously for 15 seconds to raise the undercarriage, a procedure that had 'sprog' pilots porpoising all over the sky as they attempted to take-off. There is also a brake control lever and the gun firing button on the control column spade grip, an emergency flare release control, and even a writing pad container which is seldom used in the heat of battle.

Left: The cockpit of a Spitfire IIa which 'fitted the pilot like a glove' showing the high-tech instrument panel and controls of the day.

Above: An 'erk' polishes the Spitfire's sliding canopy. Removing specks on the perspex could save a pilot's life in combat. Note the rear-view mirror and the glazed area behind the headrest.

FIRST PATROL OF THE DAY

With the Merlin purring over at 1,000 revs, Blue leader locks the brake lever on, plugs in the R/T and oxygen leads, closes the door flap and opens the radiator. He is now ready for take-off and signals the groundcrew to unplug the trolly starter and remove the chocks. They hold on to the wing tips with their hands raised when it is clear for him to taxi out to the runway. The radio is now turned on and the flying controls are full and free. The pilot releases the brakes, eases the throttle open and zigzags the Spitfire across the grass to avoid a ground collision with the other moving aircraft. It seems to be taxiing wing down but this will be due to stiffness in one of the undercarriage legs on its first flight of the day.

Above: A Spitfire II climbs away from the airfield showing off its graceful lines and distinctive elliptical wing.

Turning into wind he goes through the take-off drill –TMPFFR; T for trim elevator nose down, rudder to starboard; M for mixture rich; P for airscrew fine pitch; F for fuel on; F for flaps up; and R for radiator open. As the glycol temperature rises, Blue leader slowly opens the throttle to +6 boost at 2,000 rpm and bounces along the grass runway. After a only a 300 yard run, 'D-Delta' slices into the air at 75 mph IAS (Indicated Air Speed). The pilot pulls on the hand brake, raises the undercarriage –watching for the red light to go on, closes the radiator and canopy and

starts climbing at 140 mph. A quick look around to see Blue 1 and 2 slipping in a loose 'vic' (vee formation) behind him before Blue leader calls the Controller.

'Hullo Long John (Sector Control) Blue section airborne'.

Long John acknowledges the call with, 'Blue two, stand by for 'Pip-Squeak' in one-five seconds.' From the scramble call to airborne was three minutes 42 seconds!

At the start of the Battle, some Spitfires have been fitted with an IFF (Identification Friend or Foe) device that bounces a larger radar pulse than it received giving a larger 'blip' on the radar screens that identify it as a friendly aircraft. As not all the aircraft have IFF, and when they do, it is not always reliable, High-Frequency Direction-Finding, known as 'Pip-Squeak' is another high tech-aid available for the first time to ground controllers guiding the fighters into battle. A remote wireless contactor dial located near the oxygen socket is divided into four sections each marking 15 second transmissions. When switched on it transmits a high-pitched 15 second 'squeak'

which drowns out all R/T conversation, but is picked up by ground stations which can 'fix' the Spitfire's position. Only one of the section's aircraft is required to 'Pip-Squeak' to fix the formations position. If its pilot forgets to switch on the transmitter, Sector Control would ask, 'Is your cockerel crowing?'

As the section settles down to steady 2,000 feet per minute climb at 180 mph that will take it to 20,000 ft in less than 10 minutes, the R/T crackles into life. 'Diamond Blue section , vector one six zero. Angels three two.'

Above 20,000 ft, the maximum rate of climb drops to 1,000 feet per minute at 140 mph as Blue leader's head turns constantly searching above, below, left, right, behind and into the sun now high in the east. The First World War adage 'Beware the Hun in the Sun' has real meaning up here. The soft silk scarf stops his neck from chafing against the straps and Mae West which at this altitude feels like sandpaper. The oxygen is now full on and its extremely cold in the cockpit. There is continual chatter on the R/T but its from other aircraft in other parts of the sky. Then the disjointed voice of Long John Controller calls Blue section.

'Thirty plus bogeys east of Boulogne. Continue patrol.'

As the Spitfires stagger up to their ceiling of 32,000 feet, their rate of climb is down to 400 feet per minute and the speed drops to 110 mph. Not ideal for a dogfight with a Bf 109! The climb has taken almost 25 minutes.

Most of southern England, the English Channel and part of northern France can be seen in the morning sunlight from this height, but no enemy aircraft. The canopy is beginning to ice up. There is a windscreen de-icing spray but if it is not tested at lower altitudes, the nozzle is usually frozen solid when it's needed. By now the pilot's stomach is distended with the tight Sutton Harness biting into him as he belches on the neat oxygen. But at least the Messerschmitts are not going to have a height advantage now. The section has opened out into a looser vic with Blue three weaving around the sky as 'A E Charles Esq' or 'tail-end Charlie'. Suddenly Blue leader is snapped out of his reverie by the R/T.

'Blue two, Bandits at four o'clock. Angels two five.'

The milled rings surrounding the firing button on the Dunlop spade grip are twisted

Above: After an abortive high-level patrol over the South coast, Spitfire Ia AR213 returns to the airfield with its undercarriage and flaps down.

ALLOWING LEAD FOR MOVING TARGETS

The Spitfire Mark I's GM.2 reflector sight was the first to use stadiometric ranging to tell the pilot exactly when the target was at a predetermined range and accurately allow for deflection and bullet drop.

100 mph

2¹/₂ radii

250 mph

1¹/₂ radii

150 mph
90° off

300 mph
30° off

2 radii

250 mph
55° off

from 'Safe' to 'Fire' and he turns on the GM.2 reflector sight. This projects a illuminated graticule on to a glass screen, the size of which can be varied according to the size of the target so that the pilot can see when he is within range. Blue leader sets it for a Bf 109 with a 20 degree deflection. Eyes strain to see the bogeys which Blue leader picks up as individual dots heading towards the French coast at high speed. He calls

'Blue section. Buster. Go to full throttle'. The section dives towards the German fighters keeping a wary eye on their mirrors in case they have been lured into a trap. As the speed builds up to almost 400 mph, the fabric-covered ailerons balloon and the controls get progressively heavier. They are not going to catch the Messerschmitts before they are over their bases in occupied France so Blue leader calls off the chase.

Another call from the Controller. 'Blue section pancake, pancake.' Return to base and land immediately.

Finding the airfield is not that easy. Most 'sprog' pilots have only had time for one sector familiarisation flight since they were posted to the squadron. Then the airfield has been camouflaged with hedges 'painted'

across the runways to merge with the surrounding countryside. To further confuse the enemy, and the inexperienced, 'Q-sites' or dummy airfields are positioned close to real sector stations. Blue leader has been in the Battle for almost a month and navigates his section into the circuit with ease.

With the canopy locked open, he throttles back to 140 mph and carries out the vital landing actions –UMPF; U for undercarriage down, watch for the green light and the indicator peg in the wing; M for mixture rich; P for airscrew pitch coarse; F for flaps down. Due to the restricted forward view over the fighter's long nose, the 'Spitfire Curve' using its excellent low-speed handling is the recommended way of landing, but only when it is mastered. Blue leader reduced his speed to 85 mph and adjusts his seat as high as possible as he expertly curves off the downwind leg to make his final approach into wind. With a touch of sideslip he makes a three point landing with his head stuck out of the cockpit bringing 'D-Delta' to a stop in less than 250 yards without touching the brakes. He taxies back to the dispersal to be greeted by his groundcrew, allows the Merlin to idle for a few seconds before pulling the slow-

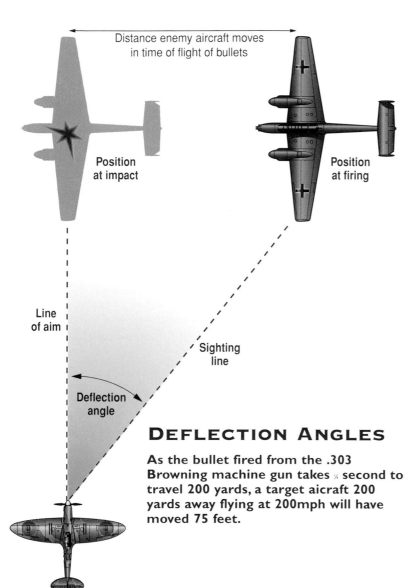

Distance enemy aircraft moves
in time of flight of bullets

Position
at impact

Position
at firing

Line
of aim

Sighting
line

Deflection
angle

DEFLECTION ANGLES

As the bullet fired from the .303
Browning machine gun takes ¼ second to
travel 200 yards, a target aicraft 200
yards away flying at 200mph will have
moved 75 feet.

SIGHT VIEWS

The gap of the horizontal graticules
seen in the reflector sight can be
adjusted by the pilot to equal the
wingspan of enemy fighters or bombers.
When the target filled the gap he then
knew the range when his fire would be
most effective allowing for bullet drop.

500 yards.
No deflection and
allowance for
bullet drop

*Above: A Bf 109 seen at 500 yards with no
deflection but allowance for bullet drop.*

150 yards.
No deflection

*Above: A Bf 109 at 150 yards with no
deflection necessary.*

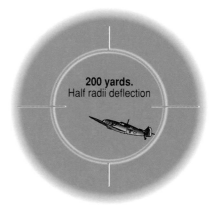

200 yards.
Half radii deflection

*Above: A Do 217 climbing at 45 degrees at a
range of 200 yards with ½ radii deflection*

running cut-out to bring the prop to a halt.
Fuel cocks and ignition switches off. Blue
section has been airborne for 55 minutes but
seen no action.

Blue leader's fitter is up on the wing asking
the pilot if there are any problems with the
engine while a petrol bowser moves into
position to pump the tanks full of 100 octane
petrol, 48 gallons in the top tank and 37 in
the bottom tank. On a cross-country cruise,
full tanks will give a maximum range of
nearly 500 miles or an endurance of two
hours. In the heat of combat, Spitfire pilots
are lucky if they can keep flying for more
than 45 minutes. There is no need for the
armourers as the canvas patches over the gun
muzzles are still intact.

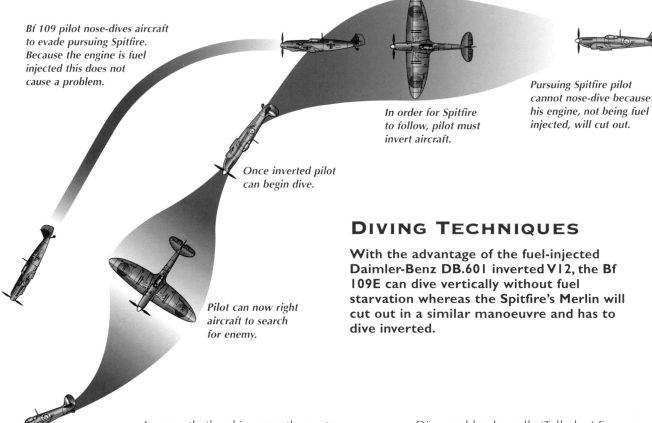

Bf 109 pilot nose-dives aircraft to evade pursuing Spitfire. Because the engine is fuel injected this does not cause a problem.

In order for Spitfire to follow, pilot must invert aircraft.

Pursuing Spitfire pilot cannot nose-dive because his engine, not being fuel injected, will cut out.

Once inverted pilot can begin dive.

Pilot can now right aircraft to search for enemy.

Spitfire pilot has now lost enemy aircraft.

DIVING TECHNIQUES

With the advantage of the fuel-injected Daimler-Benz DB.601 inverted V12, the Bf 109E can dive vertically without fuel starvation whereas the Spitfire's Merlin will cut out in a similar manoeuvre and has to dive inverted.

Apparently the skies over the sector are clear of enemy aircraft –for the time being, enabling pilots to snatch a late breakfast before the next call that comes at 10.35 hours.

'Scramble Diamond Squadron. Patrol Brighton. Angels two five.'

Twelve Spitfires accelerate across the grass airfield. Blue leader gathers his section together and slides into position behind Red section climbing steeply to 25,000 feet.

'Long John to Diamond leader. 75 plus crossing towards Hastings. Angels one five up.'

When Diamond leader has reported his position and height, the Controller's voice comes over the R/T again. 'Another 50 plus bogeys heading towards Isle of Wight. Vector two one zero, angels two two. No smoking!' This last instruction is to stay low enough to avoid creating tell-tale vapour trails which will give their position away.

Gun sights turned on, gun buttons to 'fire'.

'Diamond leader, your target passing port to starboard, range five miles. Watch out for high 'snappers' (enemy fighters).'

Suddenly the several calls come over the R/T. 'Ack-Ack at three o'clock.' 'Hurricanes joining low to port.'

'Bandits on the nose'.

Diamond leader calls 'Tally-ho.' Enemy sighted. 'Diamond leader to Diamond aircraft. Go for the snappers. Pick your own targets.'

Blue One calls for his number two to close-up and Blue Three to weave and watch their rears. The solid mass of German bombers is making for the radar station at Ventnor, keeping close together for protection as the Hurricanes wade into the formation. A Spitfire flashes past Blue leader twisting and turning as the Bf 109 on his tail manoeuvres for a lethal shot. Going to buster, Blue leader fires a quick burst at the German fighter. Although out of range, it breaks the German pilot's concentration giving his target the chance to roll over on his back into a steep dive and out of trouble. By now Blue section is down amongst the top layer of bombers. A Ju 88 comes into his sights.

A five second burst finds its target. Pieces break off and oily smoke plumes out of the bomber's starboard engine. It jettisons its bombs and falls into a steep slow-motion spiral. Two parachutes stream out of its fuselage. Blue leader has no time to watch it crash into the sea as tracer zips past his cockpit.

'Blue leader look out behind'. The call is too late. He has been 'bounced'. Two Bf 109s

Above: Groundcrews hurry to refuel and re-arm these 66 Sqn Spitfire Is. Note the guns have been fired and broken canvas patches over the muzzles.

Left: Three sections of 222 Sqn's Spitfires take-off, some with wheels already retracting, over a parked Spitfire of 610 Sqn from an 11 Group airfield.

Above: RAF fighter pilots shot down in the 'drink' during the Battle of Britain were lucky to be picked up by one of the few Walrus amphibians, known as 'Shagbags', available for air-sea rescue duties.

Below: The G.42B cine camera-gun fitted in the port wing root of Battle of Britain Spitfire Is and IIs, which proved unreliable during combat.

falling out of the sun are on his tail. At the same time Blue Two calls that he has been hit by the same pair and is on fire. One of the Messerschmitts overshoots as Blue leader sideslips beneath the second Bf 109 and half rolls into a steep 4g turn.

Initially the German pilot matches the turn, but whenever he gets the Spitfire in his sights, the Bf 109's low speed wing slots flip open causing the ailerons to snatch and spoil his aim. Now on the verge of blacking out, Blue leader reverses the turn to bring him on the '109's tail. A quick squirt with eight Brownings hits the snapper's outer wing and makes it pull up into a slow but steep climb. Bouncing around in its slipstream, the Spitfire cannot get up to a steep enough angle to bring its guns to bear but Blue Three has stuck

with his leader and dives out of the sun to deliver the *coup de grace*. A flash of flame streams from the engine and the Bf 109 rolls over on its back and plunges into the sea. There is no sign of a parachute.

The dogfight, which lasted less than ten minutes, leaves the Spitfires over mid-Channel at low level and vulnerable to being bounced again. It's time to go home. Diving to sea level heading for the English coast, Blue leader notices two Spitfires circling at 1,000 feet above the waves. One is Diamond leader keeping watch over a pilot in the drink. Blue Two has parachuted from his burning aircraft and his yellow Mae West is spotted by Red Section. They report his position and call out an air sea rescue Walrus amphibian. As the 'gravy state' (available fuel) of all the Spitfires is extremely low, they have to leave before the 'Shagbag' arrives.

As the Merlin clanks to a stop after a hectic 40 minutes in the air, armourers and refuellers swarm over 'D-Delta' as the fitter and rigger check the engine and airframe. A cannon shell has punched a hole in the rudder but missed anything vital. Close! It can be patched up in less than an hour. The pilots are met at the dispersal hut by 'Spy', the Intelligence Officer, a former pilot himself, who wants an accurate debrief of the fight. Blue leader 'claims' one 'kill' and a 'share' but as his camera gun has failed to work, he will have to wait for confirmation by two other sources.

Blue two is picked up alive but has severe burns to the face and hands. He never liked wearing gloves or goggles and will spend the

The rigger pulls the battery trolley's lead out as the Spitfire IIs 1,175hp Rolls-Royce Merlin XII as it bursts into life.

Left: A Luftwaffe Heinkel He 111H *over the River Thames passing through east central London with Limehouse off its starboard wingtip*

rest of the year in hospital. A 'sprog' pilot is missing.

As raids totalling 250 aircraft build up during the day, Diamond Squadron is held back until the last moment. Just before 14.30, the scramble call comes through. As the pilots race for their aircraft, air raid sirens begin to wail. Groundcrews whip the chocks away and as the Spitfires taxi for take-off the R/T crackles into life.

'Diamond aircraft, 'panic' 'panic' (air raid alert), get airborne immediately. Bandits in your sector.'

Aircraft get in each other's way as throttles are pushed through the 'gate' for take-off. Seven Spitfires are airborne before the first stick of bombs explodes on the airfield. The blast catches a straggler, blowing the Spitfire upside down. It slides across the grass runway

'THE HUN IN THE SUN'

The classic 'Hun in the sun' position employed by *Schwarms* – 'finger four' formations of *Luftwaffe* Bf 109s often caught RAF Spitfires flying in First World War 'vic' formation, which had no 'tail-end charlie', unaware as the British fighters dived on lower formations of 'unprotected' German bombers.

on its back waving its legs in the air before coming to rest with its nose through the boundary hedge. The rest of the squadron is scrambling for height trying to avoid mid-air collisions with friend and foe. A Do 217 appears a few feet above Blue leader's head. The slipstream hits his aircraft like a bow wave. A quick squirt but no time to

Delta' enables its pilot to position the Spitfire slightly below and behind the yellow nosed German in a shallow dive which takes his speed to 360 mph. It seems an age before he closes within 250 yards of his unsuspecting prey. A short burst, the recoil feels like hitting a brick wall and the Bf 109 noses down into a vertical dive. The Spitfire pilot rolls on his back and follows it down. The German may

see the results. The enemy aircraft are already being chased by Hurricanes and a number of aircraft are falling in flames.

Having managed to climb to 15,000 feet unscathed, Blue leader calls to his number two but gets no reply. The R/T is full of near-hysterical shouts of warning, fear and the last words of dying pilots. The Controller can do little at this stage other than divert his airborne squadrons away from airfields under attack as they call in with low 'gravy states'. Luckily the escorting Bf 109s have stuck close to the bombers giving them no chance of bouncing the defending fighters out the sun –their favourite tactic. Blue leader spots one them turning for home as its fuel runs low. The Messerschmitt's range is even less than that of the Spitfire. The superb handling of 'D-

Left: Clipped inside the door flap of the Spitfire I and II was a crowbar which could be used to smash open the canopy in an emergency.

Above: An He 111H of KG.1 from Luftflotte 2 was shot down by a British fighter and crash landed in a Surrey field at the height of the Battle of Britain.

pull out at the last minute and head for home, but the Messerschmitt's canopy suddenly breaks away followed by the pilot who takes to his parachute. The Bf 109 flips into a spin shedding a wing on the way down to a watery grave.

Blue leader heads back to base, which is easy to spot as smoke billows from bomb damaged hangars. The sortie lasted 35 minutes in which time several buildings were demolished, two Spitfires damaged on the ground, and 14 people killed. The pilot blown over on take-off survived with a broken arm. Two of those who got airborne are missing including Diamond leader.

The runway was still serviceable and the surviving pilots are airborne yet again less than an hour later. Another 100 plus bandits are over the 'Golf Course', the codename for Le Touquet. Green and Blue sections are vectored to intercept the raiders over Bexhill.

'Green leader to Diamond aircraft, bandits at angels one eight steering two seven zero. Lets go!'

Blue leader snatches a quick glance over his shoulder and up above. Two thousand feet overhead are a dozen silver dots caught by the sun.

'Snappers above, Diamond aircraft break! break!'

The six Spitfires scatter, heading for the fluffy clouds building in the afternoon heat. Another chance for a mid-air collision. Thirty seconds later Blue leader breaks out the cloud. He is alone. No Spitfires, Messerschmitts or 100 plus bombers to be seen. He goes to buster and climbs fast to get the sun behind him. Something catches the corner of his eye. The quick change of direction combined with lack of oxygen, the force of 'G' and fatigue, make him black out for a few seconds. He regains consciousness in a steep climb, on the edge of stalling. The Spitfire flicks into a spin. The pilot vaguely remembers that the 'Spitfires Pilot's Notes' state that 'flick manoeuvres are not permitted' and that 'spinning is only permitted by pilots who have written permission from the CO!'

Luckily, at 28,000 feet there is plenty of room to recover and the Spitfire is again under full control after losing only 7,500 feet. The Controller is on the R/T reporting bandits over Tunbridge Wells at angels two zero. Blue leader sees a loose formation of four bombers, one of which is streaming smoke out of one engine. Another quick look around. No 'Huns in the sun' this time. Diving on the wounded straggler, he notices that the rear gun hangs down, motionless. The gunner must be wounded. The bomber, now

Above: A Spitfire IIa bearing the markings of 266 (Rhodesia) Sqn which was based at Wittering in 12 Group, zooms low over the airfield.

Left: A Bf 109E of JG.51 shot down on the outskirts of London during the latter phase of the Battle of Britain broke its back hitting a haystack.

recognisable as an He 111, rapidly fills the gun sight. He fires a long burst. The bomber lurches to one side and the Spitfire overshoots. The pilot is obviously still alive. He banks hard to starboard to bring 'D-Delta' behind and below the Heinkel.

Pressing the 'tit' for the second time, an explosion beneath his Spitfire nearly blows him onto his back. He fights to regain control.

A small cloud of black smoke drifts away. An anti-aircraft salvo aimed at the leading pair of German bombers almost a mile ahead, is way off target. Blue leader checks for damage and tells Control what he thinks of the ack-ack battery. The He 111 flies on with its damaged engine, but rapidly losing height. The Spitfire fires another long burst, starting from 500 yards out. Tracer strikes the bomber, but still it

SCHWARM FORMATION

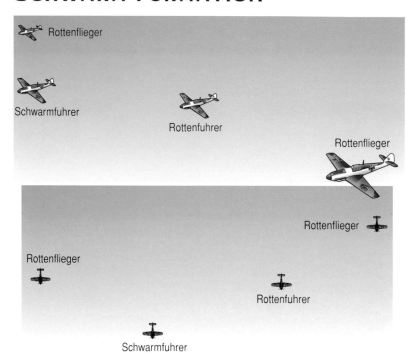

Rottenflieger

Schwarmfuhrer

Rottenfuhrer

Rottenflieger

Rottenflieger

Rottenflieger

Rottenfuhrer

Schwarmfuhrer

The Schwarm or 'Four Finger' formation was developed by the Condor Legion during the Spanish Civil War and adopted by the *Luftwaffe*. It was later adopted by the RAF after the weakness of pre-war British tactics was exposed during the Battle of Britain.

Below: Ending up in a similar predicament to the Messerschmitt, this Spitfire Ia of 92 Sqn was bent but repairable after making a forced landing.

stays in the air. Suddenly there is a hiss of compressed air. Out of ammunition: a sitting target.

It has been a frustrating and draining sortie. Back on the ground he discovers that the squadron can only claim one confirmed kill, but all the Spitfire pilots return safely. Blue leader's 'lucky' Heinkel had made a crash landing near Hastings. Two of the crew are dead and another wounded. It has more than 50 bullet holes in it.

Having spent hours in tight cockpits alternately frozen or sweating under the summer sun, with adrenaline pumping during combat, or frustrated by lack of targets, the remaining pilots of Diamond Squadron have been at readiness for almost 12 hours.

Fortified by strong NAAFI tea and greasy wads (sandwiches), there is still another three hours of daylight and other raids are expected. 'Spy' grabs the opportunity to 'interrogate' the battle weary pilots.

When another scramble call comes through at 17.20 hours, Red and Blue sections are again ordered into combat. They are 'paired' with nine Spitfires of Kingfisher Squadron for a readiness patrol on the Maidstone patrol line at angels one eight. At this time of day Messerschmitt Bf 110s carrying 550 lb bombs are in the habit of making sneak hit and run raids across Kent and the Controller is warning that 50 plus bandits are forming up over Cap Gris Nez. Heading across the Channel, the twin-engined Messerschmitts

split into three small formations and dive low under the radar. Kingfisher aircraft are ordered to climb to angels three zero to watch out for escorting Bf 109s while Diamond sections are vectored to the leading Bf 110 raiders.

Blue leader leads his section into a dive out of the lowering sun to 10,000 feet where six pairs of eyes search for the camouflaged fighter-bombers. As a long-range escort fighter, the Bf 110 'Destroyer' has been a failure and suffered heavy losses from the much faster and more agile Spitfires. This should be a picnic. But at low level their small formations are difficult to spot against the patchwork fields of Southeast England. The call comes from Blue Two, 'Four bandits 11 o'clock low.'

'Blue section Tally-ho.. Pick a winner and watch your backs.'

Blue leader leads the charge firing a long burst into one of the slim two-seaters as it fills his sights. Pieces of cockpit break away as it rears up, stalls and falls towards the ground.

Less than a mile ahead is another *Schwarm* of four Germans who jettison their bombs and scatter. Blue leader tries to cut one them off as it attempts to escape by diving to tree top level over the North Downs. Although slower than the Spitfire, the dive accelerates the Bf 110 to over 300 mph and Blue leader struggles to overtake it. He is forced to stay slightly above the skidding Destroyer when his windscreen is suddenly covered with opaque liquid –ethylene glycol coolant. In the thrill of the chase he has committed a cardinal sin. He has forgotten the '110's rear gunner whose lucky burst from his single 7.9 mm machine gun has hit the mark. Blinded, close to the ground at 300 mph and with the enemy gunner still taking pot shots at him, Blue leader hits the R/T button, 'Blue leader to Blue Two, I've been hit. Can you cover me?'

'Blue Two. I see you. Break to starboard.'

With engine temperatures rising, Blue leader knocks out the small clear-view panel on the right hand of the canopy and uses his forward speed to zoom upwards in a desperate quest to gain height before the Merlin bursts into flame. Levelling out at 2,000 feet, the pilot trims nose down, closes the throttle, switches off the magnetos and fuel cocks and feathers the windmilling prop. With the canopy fully open letting in the smell of hot engine, Blue leader searches for a likely spot for an emergency landing.

Luckily, there are a number of recently harvested corn fields to choose from for a wheels up landing. He pushes the nose down

to maintain a glide speed of 120 mph as he turns into wind, aims at a flat-looking field and tightens his safety straps. A bit high. He pushes the nose down to increase speed. Better too fast than too slow and stall. The Spitfire strikes the ground at 100 mph, bounces once then slides over the corn stubble towards a stone drinking trough in the corner of the field. The port wing tip hits the trough sending 'D-Delta' into a jarring ground loop, wrenching his shoulder, before it grinds to a halt in a cloud of dust and steam. He cuts his lip open on the gun sight. The pilot hits the Quick Release box and throws himself out of the hot cockpit.

The next day he is passed 'fit for flying' while the remains of D-Delta are loaded on a 'Queen Mary' transporter for its journey to a CRO depot. Three weeks later it will be returned to Fighter Command in new condition but before that, Diamond Squadron and its surviving pilots are stood down and sent north to rest.

Above: The scene in 11 Group's Operations Room showing WAAF plotters, and squadrons available at Sector Stations and their satellite airfields.

THE ENEMY
BANDITS

During the Battle of Britain the RAF was fighting an experienced, professional and determined adversary. Developed as an undercover 'sports' flying organisation in the late 1920s, the *Luftwaffe* was able to be very selective in both its equipment and personnel. New training aircraft were developed to train 'private' pilots belonging to the German Sport Aviation Association. Bombers were developed from long-range commercial transports designed for Germany's airline Lufthansa, and fighters were bred from high-performance aerobatic sports aircraft.

By 1930, some 50,000 people had enrolled in German aviation societies and clubs. The Hitler Youth organisation with its emphasis on physical fitness and discipline proved to be an ideal source of potential aircrew. After initial experience with gliding clubs of the *National Sozialische Flieger Korps*, the best were selected for training with either the German Air Transport School, or at a secret military aviation training centre in Russia.

All pretence of a 'private and commercial' flying organisation was swept aside when the existence of the *Luftwaffe* was officially revealed by Adolf Hitler in 1935 by which time the German Air Force had ordered a total of 4,000 new combat aircraft. A year later, the Spanish Civil War broke out and the fledgling *Luftwaffe* wasted no time in forming

Right: Dornier Do 17Z-2 medium bombers of KG.76 took part in a number of low-level raids on Fighter Command airfields in August 1940 but suffered heavy casualties in the process.

an operational unit to evaluate its new equipment in combat. The Condor Legion, ostensibly formed in response to a request by Spain's right wing rebels for technical assistance, proved to be invaluable not only for General Franco's victorious Nationalists, but for the *Luftwaffe's* preparation and planning for the greater conflict to come.

By the time Germany invaded Poland, the *Luftwaffe* was the largest and most capable air force in the world. It was highly professional and had a monthly intake of 800 new pilots.

Its elite were the medium bomber crews who had over 250 hours of flying training plus Link simulator time. They flew the Heinkel He 111 and Dornier Do 17, early versions of which were used by the Condor Legion. Both types were introduced into service with Lufthansa in the mid-1930s, thinly disguised as high-speed courier aircraft, but they suffered badly at the hands of RAF Fighter Command during the Battle of Britain. More successful was the high performance Ju 88 which could match the Spitfire's speed in a dive.

Below: During the invasions of Poland and France, Skuka dive bombers built up a fearsome reputation but were decimated by RAF fighters. This Ju 87B of KG.2 crash landed near Chichester in August killing its two man crew.

Left: The exposed 'glasshouse' nose of the Heinkel He 111H medium bomber which had a crew of five and was armed with five 7.9 mm machine guns.

Above: Messerschmitt Bf 110Cs of I/ZG.2 at an airfield in France. The Destroyer began the Battle of Britain as a bomber escort but finished as a fighter-bomber escorted by Bf 109s.

The Junkers Ju 87 dive bomber had been used to great affect in Spain and the Stuka's reputation as a terror weapon grew during the *Blitzkrieg* of Poland and the Low Countries. However, the *Luftwaffe* had gained almost complete air superiority during these campaigns, something it never achieved during the Battle of Britain. Consequently, formations of the slow, lightly armed Ju 87 were decimated by RAF fighters and soon withdrawn from the Battle.

At the beginning of the war, the *Luftwaffe's* elite fighter units were equipped with the Messerschmitt Bf 110 *Zerstörer* (Destroyer) long-range escort fighter. On paper, the slim twin-engined two-seater had a similar performance to that of the Hurricane but until the Battle of Britain, it had only fought against outdated biplane fighters in Poland, Norway and the Low Countries. Employed as a bomber escort in the early phases of the Battle of Britain, the Bf 110C's lack of agility

Left: The Messerschmitt Bf 108 Taifun, an all-metal high-performance four-seat monoplane designed in 1933, was the forerunner of the Bf 109 fighter.

Right: Luftwaffe armourers re-arming a Bf 110C Destroyer in France with 1,000 rounds of 7.92 mm ammunition for each of its four MG 17 machine guns.

Left: The Bf 109E which first flew in 1939, fought in the Battle of Britain. Note the pilot's restricted visibility, square wingtips and the twin nose-mounted 7.9 mm machine guns.

Below: A view into the 'greenhouse' cockpit of the Bf 109E, a compact battle-station with easy to read intruments and easy to reach switches and controls.

and weak twin-tail structure led to it being outclassed by British fighters. It ended the Battle as a light bomber, having to be escorted by the Bf 109.

What was to prove the *Luftwaffe's* most successful fighter was undoubtedly the single-engine Messerschmitt Bf 109 which was built in larger numbers than any other combat aircraft in the Second World War. A contemporary of the Hurricane, the Bf 109E had the same performance as the Spitfire Ia and in the right hands there was little to choose between the two fighters.

On the plus side was the Bf 109's superb fuel-injected 1,100 hp Daimler-Benz DB.600 inverted V12 engine which gave it instantaneous throttle response and enabled it to perform flick manoeuvres and negative g dives without the engine cutting out from fuel starvation. The Bf 109 could climb and dive more steeply than the Spitfire and match it in the turn too. However, it became progressively heavier to control in high speed dives, and high g pullouts were prone to collapse the wings, which were not as strong as those of the Spitfire. The Messerschmitt also had less lateral control at high speeds. Another disadvantage was its cramped

cockpit and restricted visibility due to the canopy's flat-topped 'greenhouse' framework, and lack of any rear-view glazing Visibility was further restricted by an 8 mm armour plate fitted behind the headrest and curved over the pilot's head. The canopy also hinged sideways and could not be opened during take-off and landing, or in an emergency. It was fitted with a canopy jettison device, but this was prone to jam when damaged. The Bf 109's controls and instruments were well laid out and fell easy to hand. The manual flaps were simple to operate and unaffected by damage to the hydraulics system. The single 88 gallon self-sealing fuel tank was installed directly behind the pilot's seat.

Although it had excellent low speed handling the Messerschmitt's narrow, spindly undercarriage legs gave novice pilots a difficult time during training. Most student pilots had at least 100 flying hours built up over a year before they had their first flight in the '109. The Bf 109 *Emil* outgunned the Spitfire Ia with a pair of nose-mounted 7.9 mm MG 17 machine guns and two wing-mounted 20 mm MG FF cannon. The pilot could fire the cannon or machine guns separately, or all four guns at once.

Above: A Bf 109E-3 showing its 1,100hp inverted V12 Daimler-Benz DB.601A engine, and 'greenhouse' cockpit.

THE COMMANDERS

Commander-in-chief of the *Luftwaffe* from its inception until the last days of the war was *Reichmarshall* Hermann Göring, World War One 'ace' and Hitler's designated successor. At the beginning of the Battle of Britain, Göring's right-hand men were Germany's highest scoring 'ace' to survive World War I, *Generaloberst* Ernst Udet, credited with 62 victories, and head of the *Luftwaffe's* Technical Department, the former Lufthansa boss *Feldmarschall* Erhard Milch, head of the Air Ministry. These two men were to fall out before the Battle was over in much the same way as the RAF's Air Vice-Marshals Park and Leigh-Mallory.

Opposing Fighter Command in July 1940 were three *Luftwaffe* Air Fleets. *Luftflotte* 2 based in Northeast France and the Low Countries was commanded by the very capable *Feldmarschall* Albrecht 'Smiling Albert' Kesselring, a former Army officer who transferred to the embryo *Luftwaffe* in 1933. *Luftflotte* 3 in central France was led by *Feldmarschall* Hugo Sperrle, another World War One veteran and former commander of the Condor Legion. Commanding the smaller *Luftflotte* 5 based in Norway and Denmark was *Generaloberst* Hans-Jurgan Stumpff, a former Lufthansa personnel director and *Luftwaffe* Chief-of-Staff.

Appointed *Kanalkampfuhrer* (Channel Battle Leader) for *Alderangriff* (Eagle Attack) was *Oberst* Johannes Fink whose deputy, the Channel Fighter Leader, was *Oberst* 'Uncle' Theo Osterkamp, another First World War ace with 32 kills to his credit. By the end of the Battle of Britain he had added six more kills to his score flying Bf 109s.

Each *Luftflotte* comprised 250 –1,000 combat aircraft, a mix of fighters, bombers, and reconnaissance aircraft assigned to *Jagdfliegerfuhrers* and *Fliegerdivisions* respectively. However, as there had never been a long term strategic plan to conduct aerial warfare against Britain, Göring expected his Air Fleet Commanders to submit plans for the gaining air superiority over the RAF in the few weeks prior to Operation *Seelöwe*. Kesselring and Sperrle came up with different solutions and a compromise plan formulated by Göring was finally adopted by Hitler.

From the very beginning of the Battle there was little integration between the Air Fleets. They all had their own separate operational planning, unit briefings and radio frequencies. There was no unified ground control organisation or operational radar network Although Germany had excellent intelligence regarding the location of British airfields, port facilities and aircraft factories, many of which had been photographed from Lufthansa airliners flying into Croydon before the war, the *Luftwaffe* seriously underestimated the RAF's strength and the effectiveness of its ground control and tactics.

As the Battle continued with little sign of a *Luftwaffe* victory, experienced young fighter commanders were bought in to replace some of the veterans. These included ex-Condor Legion *Majors* Werner Molders and Adolf Galland. Molders took over Osterkamp's unit *Jagdeschwader* (Fighter Group) 51 and Galland was given command of JG.26, both part of *Luftflotte* 2. Both these Bf 109 pilots would add to their Spanish Civil War scores

Left: A German propaganda picture of a captured Spitfire I being pursued by a Bf 109E published during the Battle of Britain.

and end the battle with 54 and 52 kills respectively. The top scoring *Luftwaffe* 'ace' was the commander of *Luftflotte* 3's JG.2, *Major* Helmut Wick who was shot down over the Channel minutes after claiming his 56th victim by Spitfires of 609 Sqn on 28 November 1940.

The Bf 109's main disadvantage during the Battle was its limited range. By the time the Messerschmitts had climbed above the bomber formations they were escorting across the Channel, they were almost at the point of no return. Often, they only had time to make one diving pass at the British fighters before breaking off to return to their airfields on the French coast. If they were shot down over land, German pilots would become POWs

Right: Adolf 'Dolfo' Galland with his mechanic in front of his Bf 109E during the Battle of Britain when he commanded JG.26.

Above: Adolf Galland with his old Battle of Britain foe, Stanford Tuck, who scored 105 and 29 'kills' respectively, together at the RAF Museum at Hendon after the war.

and their war would be over. However, if they ran out of fuel or were shot down over the Channel, their chance of survival was twice that of RAF pilots in the same predicament. Not only was a dinghy, colour flare bag and Very pistol standard equipment, but the *Luftwaffe* had an efficient air-sea rescue organisation based on high-speed rescue launches and He 59 floatplanes that constantly operated in the battle area during daylight hours

Some German fighter pilots complained that the RAF had bigger targets (bombers) to aim at, but most appreciated that the Spitfire was a formidable foe. 'Daddy' Molders, as he was known to his pilots, said that ' a whole mob of Spitfires fell on me like a waterfall.' Heinze Knöcke, who finished with war with 52 kills, said 'we consider shooting down a

Spitfire to be an outstanding achievement, as it actually is.' 'Dolfo' Galland's famous reply to Göring when asked what he required to gain air superiority over the RAF in September 1940 was, 'I should like an outfit of Spitfires in my group.'

Although the *Luftwaffe's* fighter pilots were blamed for loosing the battle, their ability and determination was never doubted by RAF Fighter Command. It was the over-confident *Luftwaffe* High Command led by Göring which had under-estimated Britain's air defences. It refused to admit to its mistakes and many experienced aircrew were sacrificed. For writing a letter to *Feldmarschall* Milch at the end of August, stating that he considered the RAF to be far from exhausted, Channel Fighter Leader *Oberst* Osterkamp was reduced in rank. Ernst Udet took the defeat personally and committed suicide in November 1941. He was replaced by Erhard Milch. On his return from Udet's funeral in Berlin, Werner Molders was killed when his aircraft crashed in bad weather.

Herman Göring survived the war, although his influence with Hitler waned after the failures of the Battle of Britain, Stalingrad and the air defence of Germany, all of which he blamed on his subordinates. He was captured by the Americans in 1945, put on trial at Nuremburg and sentenced to death. He cheated the hangman by committing suicide in October 1946.

AFTER THE BATTLE

Following the Battle of Britain, the Spitfire became the RAF's main fighter type. The Spitfire was the only Allied fighter to remain in continuous production throughout the whole of the Second World War. During this period its power more than doubled, its maximum speed increased by 100 mph and its rate of climb by 80 percent. Fitted with folding wings and an arrester hook, it was also adopted by the Fleet Air Arm as a shipboard fighter christened the Seafire. It served in every theatre of operations, fulfilling numerous different roles including those of high and low level reconnaissance, high-altitude interceptor, tactical fighter-bomber, and even high-speed 'hacks' for 'Top-Brass' on ground tours.

The Spitfire was the only British fighter to used operationally by the Americans: more than 600 were flown by the USAAF during the Second World War. During and immediately after the war, Spitfires and Seafires were exported to more than 25 countries, including the Soviet Union, Sweden and Syria. They were to see action again in several post-war conflicts –the Arab-Israeli war where both sides were equipped with Spitfires, French Indo-China, the Malayan Emergency and the Korean War.

The last of 34 variants of 20,351 Spitfires and 2,408 Seafires, a Seafire FR.47 powered by a 2,350hp Rolls-Royce Griffon and armed with four 20 mm cannon, left the production line in March 1949. The last flight by an RAF Spitfire operated by the Air Ministry's Temperature and Humidity (THUM) meteorological flight at Woodvale took place in June 1957.

When Spitfires were being consigned to the

Left: On display at Hendon in Battle of Britain markings of 609 Sqn to which it was delivered in October 1940, is Mk I X4590 complete with acumulator trolley starter.

Below: Spitfires 'dressed up' for the 1969 epic film, Battle of Britain, the production of which prompted a new industry in restoring dozens of Spitfires to the air.

Left: The oldest Spitfire in captivity, Mk 1 K9942 was first delivered to 72 Sqn in April 1939 before transferring to 7 OTU during the Battle of Britain. It survived and is now on display at the RAF Museum at Hendon.

Above: Spitfire Vc AR501 starred in the Battle of Britain film and is now owned and flown by the Shuttleworth Collection at Old Warden in its original 310 (Czech) Sqn markings.

Right: Spitfire PR.XI PL983 was loaned to the US Air Attache in London after the war and donated to the Shuttleworth Collection. After restoration it was sold in France and is now flying in Florida.

Left: Spitfire IXc MH434 credited with a number of 'kills' when flying with 222 Sqn in 1944, was restored for the film and flown in Belgian Air Force colours for the 40th anniversary of the BAF's 31 Sqn in 1994.

Below: MT818 was the only Spitfire, a Mk VIII, to be converted to a two-seater by Vickers-Armstrong in 1946 and has been flying ever since. Owned by Harrier test pilot John Fairey, it is currently airworthy in the USA.

scrap heap by the hundreds in the late 1950s, and handful remained airworthy in the Britain, most of which were in private ownership, but this was to change. During the mid-1960s, the James Bond film producer Harry Saltzmann was planning an epic production of the Spitfire's 'finest hour' titled *Battle of Britain*. With the help of Group Captain T G 'Hamish' Mahaddie, a former Bomber Command pilot, a total of 27 Spitfires eventually 'starred' in the 1969 production. No less than 12 of these took part in the dramatic flying sequences. Some were already active but others had to be rescued from museums and maintenance units to be restored to fly. The film was a boost for the Spitfire restoration 'industry' and there are now more than 50 airworthy examples flying in the Britain, America, Holland, Sweden, Australia, Israel, South Africa and New Zealand.

Two of these are of Battle of Britain vintage, one owned by a petrol company, the other operated by the RAF's Battle of Britain Flight (BBMF).

P7350 is the world's oldest airworthy Spitfire having been delivered to 266 Sqn in August 1940. This Spitfire IIa came off worse in combat with a Bf 109 when flown by 603 Sqn in October and forced to crash land. Only three weeks later she was returned to service with 616 Sqn before moving on to 64 Sqn, the Central Gunnery School and 57 OTU at Harwarden. She is credited with 3 wartime kills. After the War, P7350 ended up in an RAF museum at Colerne before being rescued by the *Battle of Britain* film's crew. After filming was completed, she was presented to the BBMF to join three of her younger stablemates.

One of the world's most experienced Spitfire pilots is the Officer Commanding the BBMF since 1996, Squadron Leader Paul Day. After joining the RAF in 1961, S/L Day has flown 2,000 hours on the Hawker Hunter, 3,000 hours on the F.4 Phantom, 1,000 hours on the Tornado F.3, and over 500 hours on Spitfires since he joined the BBMF 20 years ago. All the BBMF pilots based at RAF Coningsby are current RAF Tornado pilots, but before they can fly the Spitfire they have to go back to basics. They are given a 25 hour course on one of the Flight's two veteran DH Chipmunks, the Tiger Moth's successor –and a 'tail-dragger'. This is followed by sorties in a Battle of Britain vintage Harvard before being permitted to fly the single seat Battle of Britain fighters. To qualify for the Spitfire, the pilots have fly at least 15 hours in the more forgiving BBMF Hurricane.

S/L Day regularly flies P7350 at air displays all over the UK and will be leading the Flight into the next century. 'Its a lovely aeroplane to fly', he says, 'much quieter than the Hurricane. The controls are beautifully harmonised, very light in pitch. But you can't fly hands-off for very long which presents a few problems for new pilots especially when

Left: Four airworthy Spitfires seen together at Goodwood, formally the Battle of Britain satellite airfield Westhampnett, in September 1998 included Mk XIVe MV293, Mk Vb EP120 and Mk IXc MH434.

Right: Spitfire XVIe RW382 was issued to 604 (County of Middlesex) Sqn RAuxAF in 1947 and restored for the Battle of Britain film. It remains airworthy in San Jose California.

Below: The last of the 'twenty-twos' the most powerful of the breed. Spitfire F.22 PK350 was sold to the Royal Rhodesian Air Force in 1951 and sold to a former RRAF pilot who restored to fly but it crashed in 1982 killing the owner.

Above: Spitfire PR.XIX PS853 was operated by the THUM unit at Woodvale until it was retired in 1957 but joined the BBMF in 1964 until it was sold in 1995 to pay for the restoration of one of Flight's Hurricanes.

crosswind limit, was designed to be flown from grass airfields where flying into wind is no problem. Ground handling can be difficult. The long taxi to a modern runway can cause the engine to overheat, and you can't see where you are going. Use of the brakes are to be avoided whenever possible. It swings to the left on take-off but its no problem to counteract. Landings can be something else. The flaps go down in one second, and its like hitting a brick wall. You have to predict the wind direction well in advance –hear what the aeroplane tells you! If you don't get this right on touchdown it can go off in any direction. It has a mind of its own. When landing on a runway the Spitfire is prone to float and respond to any gusts or crosswind. Even heat eddies from the metalled surface can effect it. Again, don't touch the brakes. Let it roll to a halt. This is why we have to have at least 2,400 feet of runway for landing. Great fun!'

they have to change hands to retract the landing gear. It has a benign stall –61kts clean, but takes 10,000 feet to recover from a spin. We don't practice it. It can also be hard work at high speed, but P7350 is restricted to 270kts.

'The main problem for us is having to use runways. The Spitfire II, which has a 10 kt

The Flight's second oldest Spitfire is Mk Vb, AB910 built in 1941 while its pair of PR.XIXs, PM631 and PS915 are former THUM Spitfires that joined the RAF's Historic Aircraft Flight, later the BBMF, in July 1957. It is therefore more than likely that at least one of Mitchell's remarkable fighters may remain airworthy on the 100th anniversary of the type's first flight in March 1936.

Above: In 1994-96 the BBMF's Spitfire Vb AB910, in the background, flew in the D-Day markings of 402 (RCAF) Sqn and Spitfire IIa P7350 in 72 (Enniskillen) Sqn colours.

Left: Spitfire XIX PM631 joined the Battle of Britain Flight in 1957 and has flown continually ever since.

Right: The Battle of Britain Memorial Flight's Spitfire Vb seen in the American 133 (Eagle) Sqn markings in 1990.

The latest colour scheme to be worn by the BBMF's Spitfire IIa P7350 is that of 'The Old Lady' of 277 (ASR) Sqn based at Hawkinge in Kent, which was presented to the RAF by the Bank of England..